NEP STUDENTS GUIDE FOR UNDERSTANDING DRAMA

A PRACTICAL RESOURCE FOR STUDENTS AND TEACHERS

DR. VISHWANATH BITE

Made with ♥ on the Notion Press Platform
www.notionpress.com

Dedicated to

My father, ***Shri K. S. Bite****,*

who taught me to be the best of whatever I want to be!

Contents

Introduction

> *"Have you ever considered how ancient heroes' struggles mirror our challenges today? Drama is not just entertainment; it is a powerful lens through which we can examine the human experience. Whether it's the tragic fall of Oedipus or the defiant stance of Antigone, drama encapsulates timeless stories that resonate with our contemporary lives. This book aims to uncover the magic and relevance of drama, offering young adults, educators, and theatre enthusiasts a comprehensive guide to understanding and appreciating this compelling art form."*

Drama holds a mirror to society, reflecting our deepest fears, hopes, and dilemmas. It can move us, provoke thought, and drive societal change. For young students navigating the complexities of high school literature or drama courses, grasping drama fundamentals can enrich their academic journey and enhance their analytical skills. This book is a valuable resource for educators and teachers, offering insights and practical tools to help foster a love for drama in their students. For amateur and theatre lovers, a deeper understanding of dramatic elements can lead to more nuanced performances and a greater appreciation of the craft.

The roots of drama stretch back to ancient times, originating in the religious festivals of Greece. These early plays were more than mere entertainment; they were community rituals that explored fundamental questions about human existence. The tragedies and comedies of ancient Greece set the stage—quite literally—for centuries of dramatic storytelling. As history unfolded, drama evolved, taking on new forms and styles. During the Renaissance, playwrights like Shakespeare expanded the boundaries of the genre, exploring complex characters and intricate plots. This period was marked by a flourishing of creative expression, where drama became a vehicle for exploring human psychology and societal norms.

Fast-forward to the modern era, drama continues to be a vibrant and dynamic form of storytelling. Contemporary playwrights experiment with structure, language, and themes, reflecting today's diverse and multifaceted world. From Broadway to local theatre productions, drama remains a vital part of our cultural landscape, continually reinventing itself to stay relevant and resonant.

This book will explore drama's rich history and various elements. Our journey begins with examining the essential components of drama, such as plot, character development, and themes. Understanding these building blocks will give you the tools to critically analyse and appreciate dramatic works. We will delve into the techniques used by playwrights to create compelling narratives and evoke emotional responses from audiences.

Next, we will explore different genres of drama, from tragedy and comedy to more contemporary forms like absurdism and realism. Each genre offers unique insights into the human condition and employs distinct stylistic conventions. By examining a variety of dramatic genres, you will gain a broader perspective on the versatility and depth of dramatic storytelling.

We will also consider the practical aspects of drama, such as staging, direction, and performance. Understanding the technical side of drama enhances your ability to interpret and appreciate the choices made by directors and actors. This section will be particularly valuable for those involved in theatre production or aspiring to perform on stage.

Throughout the book, we will include analyses of significant dramatic works and excerpts from notable plays, providing concrete examples to illustrate key concepts. These case studies will serve as inspiration and practical guides for your engagement with drama. You will learn how to dissect scenes, identify thematic elements, and appreciate the intricacies of dialogue and monologue.

Moreover, this book highlights the social and cultural impact of drama. Plays often serve as commentary on societal issues, challenging audiences to reflect on their values and beliefs. From the political activism embedded in Bertolt Brecht's work to exploring identity in Lorraine Hansberry's plays, drama can influence public discourse and inspire change. By understanding the socio-political context of dramatic works, you can deepen your appreciation of their relevance and significance.

In addition to historical and analytical insights, this book offers practical exercises and activities designed to enhance your engagement with drama. These interactive sections encourage you to apply what you've learned through writing your dramatic scenes, performing excerpts, or conducting discussions and debates about thematic elements. Engaging with drama hands-on will reinforce your understanding and foster a deeper connection to the material.

Ultimately, this book aims to demystify drama and make it accessible to readers of all backgrounds. Whether you are a student struggling to decipher the Shakespearean language, a teacher seeking innovative ways to inspire your class, or a theatre enthusiast looking to hone your performance skills, this guide provides the tools and knowledge to navigate the world of drama confidently.

As we embark on this journey together, keep an open mind and allow yourself to be moved, challenged, and inspired by the power of dramatic storytelling. Drama invites us to step into the shoes of others, to see the world through different lenses, and to confront the complexities of the human experience. By immersing yourself in the study of drama, you will become a more astute reader and viewer and a more empathetic and thoughtful individual.

So, let us begin this exploration of drama, delving into its storied past, its intricate mechanics, and its profound impact. May you discover the beauty and depth of drama, and may it ignite a lifelong passion for the theatrical arts.

CHAPTER I

Introduction to Drama

> *"Drama, a vital part of literature, captures human experiences and emotions through performance. It's a form of art that has evolved significantly over centuries, rooted in ancient traditions and shaping our understanding of storytelling and expression. This rich history of evolution connects us to the essence of drama, which lies in its ability to convey complex narratives through characters, dialogue, and staging, creating deeply immersive experiences for audiences. By examining the key elements that constitute drama, readers can better appreciate how these components work together to produce compelling narratives."*

This chapter will explore the fundamental drama concepts essential for analysing and appreciating various dramatic works. We define drama as an art form distinct from other literary genres. Next, we break down its basic elements: plot, character, dialogue, and staging, providing a framework for understanding how each piece contributes to the overall narrative. To highlight its unique qualities, we will also compare drama with non-dramatic texts like novels and poems. We will delve into the significance of performance in bringing a script to life, emphasizing the dynamic and thrilling nature of live theatre. This comprehensive overview will equip readers with the foundational knowledge to engage deeply with dramatic literature.

Definition of Drama

Drama, as a distinct literary form, has intrigued audiences for centuries. At its core, drama is an art form that tells stories through performances and scripts. To fully grasp drama's unique qualities, it is essential to break down its key components: plot, character, dialogue, and staging. Understanding these elements provides a clear framework for analysing dramatic works.

The plot is the backbone of any dramatic work, outlining the events that drive the narrative forward. A well-constructed plot typically includes exposition, rising action, climax, falling action, and resolution. The exposition introduces the setting and characters, while the rising action builds tension, leading to the climax, the story's turning point. Afterwards, the falling action de-escalates the conflict, culminating in the resolution where loose ends are tied up. For instance, in William Shakespeare's "Hamlet," the plot evolves from the ghost's revelation, leading to Hamlet's quest for revenge, reaching its peak during the play-within-a-play scene and resolving after the tragic duel.

Characters are another crucial drama component, serving as the vessels through which the story unfolds. They can be protagonists, antagonists, or supporting roles, each contributing to the progression of the plot and thematic depth. Strong character development helps the audience connect emotionally with the story. Consider Arthur Miller's "Death of a Salesman"; the protagonist, Willy Loman, is a deeply flawed character whose struggles with his identity and dreams make the narrative compelling and relatable.

Dialogue is the primary means by which characters communicate within the drama. Unlike novels, which use descriptive prose to convey thoughts and emotions, drama relies heavily on spoken words. Effective dialogue serves multiple purposes: it reveals character traits, advances the plot, and highlights themes. In Tennessee Williams' "A Streetcar Named Desire," the dialogue portrays the strained relationship between Blanche and Stanley and underscores the broader themes of illusion versus reality.

Staging, which includes the set design, lighting, costumes, and movement of actors, plays a pivotal role in bringing a script to life. These visual and physical elements create the atmosphere and context necessary for the audience to immerse themselves in the play's world. For example, the minimalist staging in Samuel Beckett's "Waiting for Godot" emphasises the existential themes and the emptiness of the characters' waiting.

To appreciate what sets drama apart from other literary forms, comparing it with non-dramatic texts such as novels and poems is helpful. Novels often delve deep into characters' thoughts and provide extensive background information through narrative descriptions. Poems, on the other hand, distil experiences and emotions into concise, often symbolic language. Drama uniquely combines elements of both but stands out through its emphasis on performance and dialogue. While a novel like "Pride and Prejudice" by Jane Austen offers rich insights into Elizabeth Bennet's internal musings, a play like Henrik Ibsen's "A Doll's House" presents Nora Helmer's struggles through her interactions and conversations with others.

Performance is intrinsic to understanding drama. The live enactment of a script breathes life into the written word, providing a dynamic experience that can vary with each performance based on actors' interpretations and directors' visions. For instance, witnessing a live performance of Lorraine Hansberry's "A Raisin in the Sun" adds layers of emotion and social commentary that might not be as palpable when reading the script alone. The actors' body language, vocal tone, and expressions contribute to conveying the full impact of the story.

Historical shifts in the definition of drama have also shaped how we perceive and analyse this art form. In ancient Greece, drama was closely linked to religious festivals and civic duty, often dealing with themes of fate and morality. Over time, these themes evolved, reflecting cultural and societal changes. During the Renaissance, playwrights like Shakespeare expanded the boundaries of drama, exploring complex human emotions and political intrigue. In the 20th century, they brought about movements such as realism, expressionism, and absurdism, each redefining what drama could convey. Realism, exemplified by Chekhov's "The Cherry Orchard," aimed to depict everyday life and socio-economic issues authentically, whereas absurdist works like Beckett's "Endgame" questioned the very nature of human existence and communication.

Understanding these evolving definitions is crucial for modern analysis. It allows us to see drama not just as a static form but as a reflection of humanity's ongoing dialogue with itself. As historical contexts shift, so do the themes and styles that dominate dramatic works, making drama a continually exciting and relevant field of study.

Importance of Drama in Literature

As an integral part of literature, drama serves numerous significant roles beyond mere entertainment. Understanding drama's cultural and educational importance enriches our appreciation for this dynamic art form and enhances our analytical skills. This subpoint aims to delve into these aspects, focusing on how drama reflects societal values, evokes emotional responses, serves as an educational tool, and connects with various academic disciplines.

Firstly, one of the most compelling functions of drama is its ability to mirror cultural and societal values. Plays often address prevalent societal issues, reflecting or critiquing the times. For example, Shakespeare's works frequently showcase societal norms and conflicts of his era, such as the class struggles in "Romeo and Juliet" or political intrigue in "Julius Caesar." These plays entertain and provide a window into their time's historical and social contexts. Modern dramas, like Arthur Miller's "The Crucible," reflect the tensions of McCarthyism in 1950s America, underscoring the enduring relevance of drama as a cultural mirror. Through these reflections, audiences gain insight into different societal issues, fostering a deeper understanding of the world around them.

Emotional resonance is another crucial aspect of drama. Unlike other literary forms, drama is performed live, creating a unique experience that directly engages the audience's emotions. The immediacy of watching characters navigate complex situations can evoke strong feelings such as empathy, anger, sadness, or joy. Take, for instance, Tennessee Williams' "A Streetcar Named Desire," which brings to life the intense emotions experienced by its characters, allowing the audience to feel Blanche DuBois's desperation and vulnerability. The shared emotional journey between the performers and the audience makes drama a powerful medium for exploring human experiences and emotions. This connection fosters a sense of empathy, as viewers are invited to understand and feel alongside the characters, making the themes and messages of the play more impactful.

Additionally, drama holds substantial educational value. It is an excellent tool for teaching literary concepts and cultivating critical thinking skills. Analysing a play requires students to consider character development, dialogue, plot structure, and thematic content. For instance, studying Sophocles' "Oedipus Rex" introduces students to dramatic irony, where the audience knows something, but the characters do not, enhancing their comprehension of narrative techniques. Beyond literary analysis, drama encourages active learning through performance. When students act out scenes, they engage deeply with the text, improving their understanding of the material and honing their communication skills. Drama also promotes collaborative learning, as performing a play necessitates teamwork, fostering cooperation and problem-solving abilities.

Moreover, drama's interdisciplinary connections broaden its educational scope. Its themes and narratives often intersect with subjects like history, psychology, and sociology, providing a multifaceted approach to learning. Historical dramas like those written by Bertolt Brecht offer insights into specific periods and events, enriching historical knowledge and understanding. Brecht's "Mother Courage and Her Children," set during the Thirty Years' War, vividly portrays war's economic and social impacts, making historical events relatable and tangible. Psychological elements in drama, seen in plays like Eugene

O'Neill's "Long Day's Journey into Night," explore the complexities of the human psyche, shedding light on mental health issues and family dynamics. Sociological themes are evident in works like Lorraine Hansberry's "A Raisin in the Sun," which examines racial discrimination and socio-economic challenges. Drama fosters a holistic educational experience that connects these disciplines and encourages critical analysis and broader thinking.

Historical Overview of Drama

Drama has been one of history's most influential cultural mediums, evolving significantly. This subpoint aims to trace that evolution, providing a richer context for understanding and analysing various dramatic works.

The earliest forms of drama emerged in ancient civilisations, each contributing uniquely to the art form's development. In Ancient Greece, the drama was deeply intertwined with religious festivals, particularly those honouring Dionysus, the god of wine and fertility. The Greeks introduced foundational elements such as tragedy and comedy, which laid the groundwork for Western dramatic traditions. Playwrights like Aeschylus, Sophocles, and Euripides explored complex human emotions and social themes, often reflecting their time's moral and philosophical inquiries.

Similarly, ancient Indian drama, represented by Sanskrit theatre, focused on performance in religious and social contexts. The Natyashastra, an ancient treatise on performing arts, describes various aspects of dramaturgy, including acting techniques, stage design, and music. Plays by Kalidasa and other notable playwrights delved into epic narratives and poetic dialogue, emphasising theatrical spectacle alongside storytelling.

The transition through historical periods saw drama adapting to the changing societal landscapes. During the medieval era, European drama took on an essentially religious character, with morality plays and mystery cycles teaching biblical stories and Christian values. These performances were community events, often held in public squares or church grounds, engaging audiences directly and fostering communal participation. Such plays not only entertained but also educated and reinforced prevailing moral frameworks.

The Renaissance marked a pivotal shift in dramatic forms, notably in England. Playwrights such as William Shakespeare and Christopher Marlowe expanded the scope of drama by blending classical influences with contemporary themes. Shakespeare's works, rich in language and diverse in genre, explored human nature, politics, and romance, making them timeless pieces still celebrated today. The blossoming of the Elizabethan theatre also led to the construction of iconic venues like The Globe, facilitating more sophisticated productions.

The 17th and 18th centuries further diversified dramatic styles across Europe. French neoclassicism, as exemplified by Molière and Racine, emphasised adherence to classical unities of time, place, and action. Meanwhile, Spanish Golden Age drama, led by figures like Lope de Vega, thrived on themes of honour and intrigue, showcasing elaborate plots and lively characters. In Japan, traditional forms such as Noh and Kabuki theatre evolved, combining dance, music, and drama in highly stylised performances that remain integral to Japanese culture.

The 19th century introduced significant movements that transformed the landscape of drama. Realism emerged as a response to the romantic and dramatic styles that preceded it, focusing on everyday life and ordinary people. Playwrights like Henrik Ibsen and Anton Chekhov depicted realistic scenarios and complex characters, prompting the audience to reflect on societal issues and personal dilemmas.

In contrast, expressionism sought to convey emotional experiences rather than realistic representations. This movement, prominent in early 20th-century Germany, employed exaggerated gestures, stark lighting, and abstract scenography to evoke psychological states. Bertolt Brecht's epic theatre, a branch of this style, aimed to provoke critical thinking and social change through techniques that reminded the audience of the artificiality of the performance.

Absurdism, another critical movement of the 20th century, challenged conventional narratives and logical structures. Playwrights like Samuel Beckett and Eugène Ionesco used illogical dialogues and bizarre scenarios to illustrate the meaninglessness of existence and the human condition's inherent absurdity. Their works often left audiences contemplating profound existential questions.

Contemporary events and societal shifts continue to shape drama. Digital technology and multimedia have introduced new forms of storytelling and performance, blurring the lines between theatre, film, and virtual reality. Modern drama frequently addresses racial inequality, gender identity, and climate change, reflecting our dynamic and interconnected world.

Moreover, global connectivity has facilitated cross-cultural exchanges, enriching dramatic traditions. Contemporary playwrights draw inspiration from diverse sources, creating works that resonate universally while addressing local contexts. For instance, Lin-Manuel Miranda's "Hamilton" blends American history with hip-hop culture, reaching a broad audience and redefining musical theatre conventions.

Types and Subtypes of Drama

Recognising drama's diverse forms is essential to understanding it. Different types of drama offer unique experiences and emotions, impacting how they are analysed and appreciated. This subpoint categorises the various forms of drama, helping readers identify and distinguish their characteristics.

The first primary type of drama to consider is tragedy. Tragedy involves serious themes and often ends in disaster for the main characters. The purpose of tragedy is to evoke a sense of pity and fear among the audience. Classic examples include works by William Shakespeare, such as "Hamlet" and "Macbeth," where the protagonists face inevitable doom due to a flaw or fate. Tragedies often explore profound human truths and moral questions, making them a significant form for deeper analysis.

Comedy, another primary form of drama, contrasts sharply with tragedy. Comedies aim to entertain and amuse, often highlighting the follies and absurdities of life. They typically end happily, resolving conflicts humorously. Shakespeare's "Much Ado About Nothing" and Oscar Wilde's "The Importance of Being Earnest" are prime examples. Comedies use wit, satire, and irony to criticise societal norms, offering audiences laughter and insight into human behaviour.

Exaggerated plots and emotional appeals characterise Melodrama. Unlike tragedy, melodramas tend to have clear distinctions between good and evil, with a focus on sensational events and heightened emotions. The stories often depict virtuous heroes battling villains, leading to dramatic rescues and happy endings. Melodramatic elements can be found in plays like George L. Aiken's adaptation of Harriet Beecher Stowe's "Uncle Tom's Cabin." While sometimes criticised for lacking subtlety, melodramas remain popular due to their ability to stir strong emotions.

In addition to these main types, drama has numerous subgenres and variations. Farce, a subtype of comedy, exaggerates situations to an extreme, creating ludicrous and improbable scenarios. Farces relies heavily on physical humour and slapstick to generate laughter. Examples include Molière's "Tartuffe" and Michael Frayn's "Noises Off." Despite their light-hearted approach, farces can critique social issues under the guise of humour.

Another intriguing variation is tragicomedy, which blends elements of both tragedy and comedy. Tragicomedies often feature dark humour and situations where tragic and comic elements coexist, reflecting the complexity of real life. Samuel Beckett's "Waiting for Godot" and Anton Chekhov's "The Cherry Orchard" illustrate this blend, presenting characters and situations that evoke laughter and sorrow.

Cultural significance dramatically influences the types and forms of drama. Different cultures shape and are shaped by their dramatic traditions. In ancient Greece, for example, tragedies were performed during religious festivals honouring Dionysus, the god of wine and fertility. These performances were entertainment and communal rituals exploring human existence and divine influence. Conversely, with its slow, ceremonial style, Japanese Noh theatre reflects the cultural emphasis on meditation and spirituality. Each culture's dramatic forms reveal insights into its values, beliefs, and social structures.

Theological and philosophical influences also play a crucial role in shaping dramatic forms. Throughout history, different worldviews have impacted the themes and styles of drama. During the medieval period in Europe, religious dramas known as morality plays depicted the battle between good and evil, teaching Christian virtues. These plays aimed to guide audiences toward moral righteousness through allegory and symbolism.

In contrast, the existential philosophy of the 20th century, with its focus on the meaninglessness and absurdity of life, led to the creation of the Theater of the Absurd. Playwrights like Samuel Beckett and Eugène Ionesco used this genre to express existentialist themes, depicting characters trapped in illogical and surreal situations. Their works challenge conventional narrative structures and encourage audiences to question reality and existence.

Moreover, political ideologies have significantly influenced dramatic forms. Bertolt Brecht's epic theatre, rooted in Marxist theory, aimed to provoke critical thinking and social change. Brecht used direct address and interrupted narrative flow to break the illusion of reality, forcing audiences to engage intellectually rather than emotionally. His works, such as "The Threepenny Opera," highlight socio-economic issues and advocate for societal transformation.

Understanding these types of drama allows readers to appreciate the genre's diversity better. Each form offers distinct ways of engaging with audiences, provoking thought, emotion, and reflection. By recognising the unique characteristics of different dramatic forms, readers can deepen their analytical skills and enrich their appreciation of dramatic works.

Analysing Drama

Analysing dramatic works can seem daunting, but with practical techniques, readers will engage more deeply with plays. One critical approach is textual analysis, which closely examines scripts' dialogue, structure, and thematic elements.

Textual analysis focuses on dialogue since it's the primary vehicle through which characters express their motivations and emotions. Pay attention to how characters speak—do they use formal language or slang? Is their speech patterned or fragmented? For instance, in Shakespeare's "Hamlet," the protagonist's soliloquies reveal his inner turmoil and philosophical ruminations. Understanding these nuances can provide insight into character development and thematic depth.

Structure is another crucial element. Plays generally follow a specific framework, often divided into acts and scenes. Familiarising oneself with standard structures, such as Shakespeare's classical five-act structure or the three-act structure famous in modern drama, can help predict and understand plot progression. Analysing how tension builds, peaks, and resolves within this framework illuminates the playwright's intent and effect.

Thematic elements are equally important. Identifying recurring motifs or symbols throughout the text can enhance one's grasp of the play's broader messages. For example, the motif of sight and blindness in Sophocles' "Oedipus Rex" underscores themes of ignorance and enlightenment. By tracking these elements, readers can uncover layers of meaning that enrich their interpretation.

Performance critique is another valuable technique that evaluates live and recorded performances. Observing different interpretations of a play reveals a range of production choices and their impacts. For example, watching two productions of Arthur Miller's "Death of a Salesman" might highlight differences in how actors portray Willy Loman's despair, altering the audience's perception of his character. Pay attention to acting, direction, set design, and lighting. How do these elements support or subvert the script?

Evaluating the actors‘ performances involves more than just watching their delivery; it includes noting their physicality, timing, and interaction with other characters. Does the actor make believable choices that remain true to the character's context? Consider also the director's vision: how has the narrative been framed visually and spatially on stage? Compelling performance critique compares these artistic decisions against the text's original intentions and sees how they illuminate or obscure specific themes.

Contextual understanding is essential for a comprehensive analysis of drama. This involves considering the historical, social, and cultural contexts in which a play was written and performed. Knowing the era's societal norms, political climate, and prevalent issues can significantly impact one's reading of a play. For instance, understanding the gender dynamics of ancient Greece adds depth to the analysis of Euripides' "Medea," where Medea's actions challenge patriarchal expectations.

Social context is equally significant. Plays often reflect or critique the societies from which they emerge. Lorraine Hansberry's "A Raisin in the Sun" explores racial discrimination and aspirations within 1950s America. Acknowledging these contexts allows readers to appreciate the play's relevance and commentary on real-world issues.

Cultural context also plays a pivotal role. Different cultures have varied traditions and storytelling methods, influencing how dramas are constructed and perceived. For example, the Japanese theatrical form Noh incorporates slow movement and minimalistic dialogue, distinctly different from Western theatrical traditions. Recognising these cultural specifics helps appreciate a play's unique aesthetic and thematic qualities.

Comparative analysis is another effective technique for deepening understanding. Comparing different works allows readers to appreciate diverse approaches and styles in drama. This could involve comparing works by the same playwright, like contrasting themes of ambition and guilt in Shakespeare's "Macbeth" with those in "Julius Caesar." Alternatively, one might compare works across different periods or cultures, such as examining existential questions in Samuel Beckett's "Waiting for Godot" alongside those in Jean-Paul Sartre's earlier work "No Exit."

Analysing similarities and differences in themes, characterisations, and narrative structures broadens one's perspective. It highlights how different playwrights address similar topics uniquely, reflecting their personal views and the contexts of their times. Through comparative analysis, readers can discern shifts in dramatic styles and concerns, enhancing their appreciation for the evolution of drama.

Drama is a dynamic and complex form of literature and performance, encompassing various elements that create a cohesive and engaging experience for both performers and audiences. Understanding the fundamental elements of drama is crucial for grasping how stories are crafted, characters are developed, and themes are conveyed. This chapter delves into the essential components of drama: plot, characters, dialogue, setting, theme, conflict, music and sound, and spectacle.

Plot: The Structure of the Story

The plot is the backbone of any dramatic work, providing the framework within which the story unfolds. The sequence of events in a play is shaped by the characters' actions, decisions, and conflicts. The plot is not merely a series of happenings, but a carefully structured narrative that creates tension, evokes emotions, and ultimately leads to a resolution.

Structure of the Plot

The traditional structure of a dramatic plot often follows a pattern known as Freytag's Pyramid, consisting of five essential parts:

Exposition: This is the introduction to the play, where the audience is introduced to the main characters, the setting, and the central conflict. The exposition provides the necessary background information that helps the audience understand the story's context. For example, in Shakespeare's *Romeo and Juliet, the exposition introduces us to the feud between the Montagues and the Capulets.*

Rising Action: Rising action involves events that complicate the initial conflict and build suspense. During this phase, characters are developed, relationships are established, and tensions escalate. Rising action keeps the audience engaged as they anticipate the outcome of the conflict.

Climax: The climax is the plot's turning point, where the central conflict reaches its highest intensity. It is a moment of excellent tension and emotional impact, often resulting in a critical decision or revelation that changes the course of the story. In *"Hamlet,"* the climax occurs when Hamlet finally confronts King Claudius, exposing his guilt.

Falling Action: The falling action follows the climax and details the consequences of the pivotal moment. It shows how the characters respond to the events of the climax, and it begins to resolve the remaining conflicts. This phase moves the story toward its conclusion, offering a glimpse of the eventual outcome.

Resolution (Denouement): The resolution is the final part of the plot, where the conflicts are resolved, and the story reaches its conclusion. It provides closure to the narrative, tying up loose ends and revealing the fate of the characters. In tragedies, the resolution often involves a downfall or catastrophe, while in comedies, it typically ends on a note of reconciliation or celebration.

Types of Plots in Drama

Different types of plots serve various purposes in drama:

Linear Plot: A linear plot follows a straightforward chronological order from beginning to end without deviating from the timeline. Most classical and traditional dramas, such as Greek tragedies, employ a linear plot structure.

Non-linear Plot: A non-linear plot does not follow a strict chronological sequence. It may involve flashbacks, flash-forwards, or parallel storylines. Modern and postmodern dramas, such as Samuel Beckett's *"Waiting for Godot,"* often use non-linear plots to explore complex themes and challenge traditional narrative structures.

Circular Plot: A circular plot begins and ends at the same point, often highlighting the cyclical nature of events or the futility of human endeavours. Eugene Ionesco's *"The Bald Soprano"* is an example of a play with a circular plot, where the ending mirrors the beginning, creating a sense of repetition and absurdity.

Characters: Protagonists, Antagonists, and Supporting Roles

Characters are the lifeblood of drama. They are the individuals who drive the plot forward, engage with the audience, and convey the themes and messages of the play. Characters in drama are more than mere representations of people; they are crafted with depth, personality, and purpose, serving as the agents through which the story unfolds.

Types of Characters

Protagonist: The protagonist is the main character around whom the story revolves. They are often the characters the audience identifies most closely and whose journey or conflict forms the play's central focus. In tragedies, the protagonist is usually a tragic hero with a fatal flaw (hamartia) that leads to their downfall, such as Oedipus in Sophocles' *"Oedipus Rex."* In comedies, the protagonist may be an ordinary person facing extraordinary circumstances, like Rosalind in Shakespeare's *"As You Like It."*

Antagonist: The antagonist is the character or force that opposes the protagonist and creates conflict. The antagonist may be a person like Iago in *"Othello,"* a group like the Capulets in *"Romeo and Juliet,"* or even an abstract force, such as fate or society. The antagonist's role is to challenge the protagonist, creating tension and driving the plot.

Supporting Roles: Supporting characters provide depth to the story, enhance the main character's development, and contribute to the unfolding of the plot. They can serve various purposes, such as comic relief (the Nurse in *"Romeo* *and Juliet"*) or a confidante (Horatio in *"Hamlet"*). They help to build the world of the play and enrich the narrative.

Foil: A foil is a character whose qualities contrast with the protagonist's, highlighting particular traits or themes. For example, in *"Hamlet,"* Laertes is a foil to Hamlet, contrasting his impulsive action with Hamlet's indecision.

Stock Characters: Stock characters are stereotypical figures representing specific types, such as the fool, the villain, the lover, or the hero. While they may lack depth, they serve essential functions in various genres, notably comedy and melodrama.

Character Development

Character development is essential to creating compelling drama. It involves defining the characters' roles and functions and giving them unique personalities, motivations, and arcs. The following elements are crucial for character development:

Backstory: A character's history provides context for their behaviour, beliefs, and motivations. A well-developed backstory adds depth and realism, making characters more relatable and believable.

Motivation: Characters must have clear motivations that drive their actions and decisions. Understanding what a character wants and why they want it is fundamental to creating believable and engaging drama.

Arc: A character arc is a character's transformation or growth throughout the story. It is often shaped by the challenges they face, their choices, and the consequences of their actions. A strong character arc adds emotional depth and resonance to the narrative.

Dialogue: The Art of Conversation in Drama

Dialogue is the primary means of communication in drama. It reveals character, advances the plot, and conveys themes and emotions. The spoken word brings the written script to life, transforming it from a static text into a dynamic performance.

Functions of Dialogue

Characterization: Dialogue reveals characters' personalities, thoughts, and emotions. How a character speaks—tone, diction, rhythm, and style—can provide insights into their background, education, social status, and psychological state.

Advancing the Plot: Dialogue moves the story forward by providing necessary information, introducing new conflicts, and revealing critical turning points. The audience learns about the characters' goals, obstacles, and relationships through dialogue.

Creating Tension and Conflict: Dialogue can create tension by highlighting conflicts between characters or introducing dramatic irony, where the audience knows more than the characters. This tension keeps the audience engaged and invested in the unfolding drama.

Establishing Mood and Atmosphere: The choice of words, phrases, and sentence structures in dialogue helps establish a scene's mood and atmosphere. For instance, sharp, terse dialogue may create a sense of urgency or hostility, while lyrical, poetic dialogue may evoke a sense of romance or nostalgia.

Techniques in Writing Effective Dialogue

Subtext: Subtext is the underlying meaning or intention behind a character's words, often conveyed indirectly. It adds complexity to the dialogue, allowing for multiple interpretations and deeper engagement. For example, a character may say, "I'm fine," but the subtext—revealed through tone, body language, or context—may suggest they are upset.

Pacing: The rhythm and flow of dialogue can affect the pace of a scene. Short, quick exchanges can create a sense of urgency or tension, while longer, reflective dialogue can slow down the pace, allowing for introspection and emotional depth.

Interruptions and Pauses: Realistic dialogue often includes interruptions, pauses, and incomplete sentences, reflecting the natural flow of conversation. These elements can enhance authenticity, reveal character dynamics, and build suspense.

Dialect and Accent: Using dialect or accent can add authenticity and richness to a character's speech, highlighting their cultural or regional background. However, it should be used sparingly to avoid stereotyping or alienating the audience.

Setting: Time and Place in Drama

The setting of a play is the environment in which the story takes place. It includes the physical location (place) and the period (time) the action occurs. The setting provides a backdrop for the action, influences the characters' behaviour, and contributes to the overall mood and tone of the play.

Components of Setting

Physical Setting: The physical setting includes the geographical location, architecture, weather, and physical objects present in the scene. It helps to create a visual context for the action, shaping the audience's perception and understanding of the story.

Temporal Setting: The temporal setting refers to the period in which the play is set, including the historical era, season, and time of day. The temporal setting can influence the characters' language, costumes, social norms, and cultural practices.

Functions of Setting

Establishing Context: The setting provides the audience context, helping them understand where and when the story occurs. This context is crucial for interpreting the characters' actions and the plot's development.

Enhancing Mood and Atmosphere: The setting can evoke specific emotions and set the tone for the play. For example, a dark, stormy night can create a sense of foreboding, while a sunny, bustling marketplace can evoke a feeling of liveliness and excitement.

Reflecting Themes: The setting can reinforce the play's themes by mirroring the characters' internal conflicts or the story's central message. For instance, in Arthur Miller's *"The Crucible,"* a Puritan village's oppressive, claustrophobic setting reflects the themes of hysteria and persecution.

Theme: The Underlying Message

The theme of a play is its central idea or underlying message. It is the deeper meaning that the playwright seeks to convey through the narrative, characters, and dialogue. Themes often explore universal human experiences, such as love, power, betrayal, or mortality, allowing audiences to connect with the story on an emotional and intellectual level.

Identifying Themes

Themes can be explicit or implicit. An explicit theme is directly stated or communicated through the characters' dialogue or actions. On the other hand, an implicit theme is suggested or implied, requiring the audience to infer its meaning based on the overall context of the play.

Functions of Theme

Providing Meaning: Themes give a play its meaning and purpose, elevating it from mere entertainment to a work of art that provokes thought, reflection, and discussion.

Creating Unity: The theme serves as a unifying element that ties together the various components of the play—plot, characters, setting, and dialogue. It provides coherence and direction to the narrative, ensuring that all elements communicate a cohesive message.

Engaging the Audience: A well-developed theme resonates with the audience, evoking empathy, challenging beliefs, and prompting self-reflection. It allows the audience to see themselves in the characters and situations, creating a deeper emotional connection to the play.

Conflict: The Driving Force of Drama

Conflict is the engine that drives the plot and creates drama. The struggle between opposing forces—whether internal or external—generates tension and keeps the audience engaged. Conflict is essential to drama because it propels the narrative forward and shapes the characters' journeys.

Types of Conflict

External Conflict: External conflict occurs between a character and an outside force, such as another character (man vs. man), society (man vs. society), nature (man vs. nature), or fate (man vs. fate). For example, in *"Macbeth,"* the external conflict is Macbeth's struggle against those threatening his reign.

Internal Conflict: Internal conflict occurs within a character's mind, often involving a moral dilemma, fear, desire, or emotional struggle (man vs. self). Hamlet's indecision about whether to avenge his father's death is a classic example of internal conflict.

Functions of Conflict

Driving the Plot: Conflict catalyses action, creating a sense of urgency and momentum. It forces characters to choose, take risks, and face consequences, driving the plot toward its climax and resolution.

Revealing Character: Conflict reveals characters' true natures by testing their values, beliefs, and resilience. How a character responds to conflict can provide insight into their personality, motivations, and growth.

Highlighting Themes: Conflict often reflects the central themes of a play, such as justice, love, power, or freedom. It allows the audience to see these themes in action, providing a deeper understanding of the playwright's message.

Music and Sound: Enhancing the Dramatic Experience

Music and sound are integral elements of drama that enhance a performance's emotional impact and overall experience. They can underscore the action, set the mood, and create a sense of rhythm and continuity.

Functions of Music and Sound

Creating Atmosphere: Music and sound effects can establish the atmosphere of a scene, evoking specific emotions or moods. For example, a sad, slow melody may create a feeling of melancholy, while an upbeat, lively tune can convey joy and celebration.

Highlighting Key Moments: Music can emphasise essential moments in the play, such as a character's entrance, a climactic confrontation, or a dramatic revelation. It can draw the audience's attention and heighten the scene's emotional impact.

Enhancing Storytelling: Music and sound effects can help to convey information, such as a change in time or location, or to suggest off-stage events (e.g., the sound of thunder indicating an approaching storm). They add layers of meaning and depth to the storytelling.

Spectacle: Visual Elements and Staging

Spectacle refers to the visual elements of a play, including the set design, costumes, lighting, and special effects. It encompasses everything the audience sees on stage, contributing to the performance's aesthetic and sensory experience.

Components of Spectacle

Set Design: The set design includes the physical environment in which the play is performed, such as the scenery, props, and furniture. A well-designed set enhances the realism of the performance, supports the narrative, and reflects the play's themes.

Costumes: Costumes help to define the characters, indicating their social status, occupation, personality, and historical period. They also contribute to the play's visual appeal and help create a sense of time and place.

Lighting: Lighting is crucial for setting the mood, directing the audience's attention, and creating visual effects. It can suggest the time of day, the weather, or the scene's emotional tone.

Special Effects: Special effects, such as smoke, fog, or projections, can add a sense of magic, mystery, or excitement to a play. They enhance the spectacle and contribute to the overall impact of the performance.

Functions of Spectacle

Engaging the Audience: Spectacle captures the audience's attention and engages their senses, making the performance more immersive and memorable.

Supporting the Narrative: Visual elements can reinforce the story, helping to convey the setting, mood, and themes. For example, a dimly lit stage with minimal props may suggest a bleak, oppressive environment. In contrast, a brightly lit stage with elaborate decorations may evoke a sense of opulence and grandeur.

Enhancing Emotional Impact: Spectacles can heighten the emotional impact of a play by creating powerful visual images that resonate with the audience. It can evoke awe, wonder, fear, or joy, adding depth and intensity to the dramatic experience.

Drama is a multifaceted genre encompassing various types and forms, each with unique characteristics, conventions, and purposes. From the solemn depths of tragedy to the joyous heights of comedy, drama reflects the breadth and complexity of the human experience. This chapter provides an overview of the primary types of drama: tragedy, comedy, tragicomedy, farce, melodrama, musical drama, and documentary drama. Each type is examined in terms of its defining features, historical evolution, and examples that illustrate its significance in the theatre.

Tragedy: The Downfall of the Hero

Tragedy is one of the oldest and most profound forms of drama, dating back to ancient Greece. It deals with serious and often sombre themes, such as human suffering, moral dilemmas, and the inevitability of fate. The central character in a tragedy, known as the tragic hero, typically experiences a downfall due to a combination of a personal flaw (hamartia), external circumstances, and fate. Tragedy aims to evoke a sense of catharsis—an emotional purging or release—in the audience, allowing them to experience and process deep emotions such as pity, fear, and empathy.

Characteristics of Tragedy

Tragic Hero: The protagonist in a tragedy is usually a noble or high-ranking individual who possesses a tragic flaw—such as pride, ambition, or jealousy—that leads to their downfall. Despite their flaws, tragic heroes often have redeeming qualities that make them relatable and evoke empathy from the audience. For example, in Shakespeare's *"Macbeth,"* Macbeth's ambition drives him to commit heinous crimes, but his inner turmoil and guilt make him a complex and tragic figure.

Conflict: Tragedy often revolves around a central conflict, whether internal (within the character) or external (between characters or between the character and fate, society, or nature). This conflict drives the plot and leads to the hero's eventual downfall.

Inevitable Downfall: An essential element of tragedy is the inevitability of the protagonist's downfall. Despite their efforts to avoid their fate, the tragic hero can ultimately not escape the consequences of their actions or the forces of destiny. This certainty creates a sense of tension and suspense.

Catharsis: Tragedy seeks to evoke a strong emotional response in the audience, particularly feelings of pity and fear. The resolution of the tragic events, often involving the hero's demise, leads to a cathartic experience, allowing the audience to release and process their emotions.

Historical Evolution of Tragedy

Classical Tragedy: Tragedy originated in ancient Greece and was heavily influenced by religious rituals and mythology. Greek tragedians like Aeschylus, Sophocles, and Euripides laid the foundations for the genre. Their plays, such as *"Oedipus Rex"* and *"Antigone,"* explored complex themes of fate, justice, and human suffering.

Elizabethan and Jacobean Tragedy: During the Renaissance, tragedy experienced a revival in England, with playwrights like William Shakespeare and Christopher

Marlowe transforming the genre. Shakespearean tragedies, such as *"Hamlet," "Othello,"* and *"King Lear,"* combined classical elements with new explorations of psychology, ambition, and human frailty.

Modern Tragedy: In the modern era, tragedy evolved to include high-born protagonists and ordinary individuals. Modern tragedies, like Arthur Miller's *"Death of a Salesman"* and Tennessee Williams' *"A Streetcar Named Desire,"* focus on social issues, personal struggles, and existential themes.

Examples of Tragedy

"Oedipus Rex" by Sophocles is a classic Greek tragedy in which King Oedipus, in his quest to avoid a prophecy, unknowingly fulfils it by killing his father and marrying his mother, leading to his tragic downfall.

"Macbeth" by William Shakespeare: A tragedy that explores the destructive power of unchecked ambition and moral corruption.

Arthur Miller's "Death of a Salesman" is a modern tragedy that portrays the downfall of Willy Loman, an ordinary man caught in the pursuit of the American Dream.

Comedy: The Light Side of Drama

In contrast to tragedy, comedy aims to entertain and amuse the audience by highlighting the lighter aspects of human life. It often involves humour, satire, and wit and ends positively, with characters overcoming obstacles and misunderstandings. Comedy celebrates human resilience, joy, and the capacity for renewal and change.

Characteristics of Comedy

Humour: Comedy relies on humour to engage and entertain the audience. This humour can take many forms, including verbal wit, physical slapstick, situational irony, and ridiculous exaggeration.

Happy Ending: Unlike tragedy, comedy typically concludes with a resolution that restores harmony, happiness, and social order. This often involves resolving romantic entanglements, misunderstandings, or conflicts, leading to reconciliation, marriage, or celebration.

Character Types: Comedies often feature a range of stock characters, such as the clever servant, the bumbling fool, the miser, the romantic couple, and the wise elder. These characters embody specific traits or stereotypes, contributing to the humour and plot.

Social Commentary: While comedies are primarily designed to entertain, they often contain underlying social commentary or satire. They may criticise social norms, human folly, or political institutions, using humour to reflect and critique.

Types of Comedy

Romantic Comedy: Focuses on love and relationships, often involving misunderstandings, mistaken identities, and obstacles that are ultimately overcome. Shakespeare's *"Much Ado About Nothing"* and Jane Austen's *"Pride and Prejudice"* are classic examples of romantic comedy.

Satirical Comedy: Uses humour to critique social norms, political institutions, or human behaviour. Oscar Wilde's *"The Importance of Being Earnest"* and George Bernard Shaw's *"Pygmalion"* are satirical comedies highlighting the absurdities of social conventions.

Farce: A subtype of comedy characterised by exaggerated situations, improbable events, and physical humour. Farces often involve slapstick, mistaken identities, and a frantic pace. Examples include *"Noises Off"* by Michael Frayn and *"The Importance of Being Earnest"* by Oscar Wilde.

Comedy of Manners: Focuses on the behaviours, customs, and attitudes of a particular social class, often using wit and satire to critique societal norms. Molière's *"The Misanthrope"* and Wilde's *"The Importance of Being Earnest"* are examples.

Examples of Comedy

"A Midsummer Night's Dream" by William Shakespeare: A romantic comedy that explores love, magic, and transformation through a series of humorous misunderstandings and enchanted situations.

"The Importance of Being Earnest" by Oscar Wilde: A satirical comedy that critiques Victorian society's obsession with appearances and social status.

"Noises Off" by Michael Frayn: A farce that portrays the chaotic behind-the-scenes of a theatrical production, filled with mistaken identities, physical comedy, and hilarious misunderstandings.

Tragicomedy: A Blend of Light and Dark

Tragicomedy is a hybrid genre that combines elements of both tragedy and comedy. It reflects the complexities of life by presenting situations that contain both serious and humorous aspects. Tragicomedies often balance despair and hope, exploring themes such as the unpredictability of fate, the ambiguity of human nature, and the coexistence of joy and suffering.

Characteristics of Tragicomedy

Mixed Tone: Tragicomedy blends the severe themes and high stakes of tragedy with the light-heartedness and humour of comedy. This creates a unique tone that can shift between tension and relief, sorrow and laughter.

Ambiguous Ending: Unlike pure tragedy or comedy, tragicomedies often have ambiguous or open-ended conclusions that do not neatly fit into either category. They may end with a mixture of loss and gain or resolution and uncertainty.

Complex Characters: Tragicomedy often features complex characters with heroic and flawed qualities. These characters may face moral dilemmas, personal conflicts, or ambiguous situations that defy simple categorisation.

Evolution of Tragicomedy

Origins in Classical Drama: Early forms of tragicomedy can be traced back to ancient Greek drama, where plays like Euripides' *"Alcestis"* contained elements of both tragedy and comedy.

Renaissance Tragicomedy: During the Renaissance, playwrights like William Shakespeare and John Fletcher experimented with tragicomedy. Shakespeare's *"The Winter's Tale"* and *"The Tempest"* are examples that combine serious themes with elements of magic, humour, and reconciliation.

Modern Tragicomedy: In modern drama, tragicomedy became famous for exploring complex and ambiguous themes. Samuel Beckett's *"Waiting for Godot"* exemplifies modern tragedy, blending existential despair with absurd humour.

Examples of Tragicomedy

"The Winter's Tale" by William Shakespeare: A tragicomedy that begins with jealousy, betrayal, and loss but concludes with reconciliation, forgiveness, and renewal.

"Waiting for Godot" by Samuel Beckett: This modern tragicomedy explores the existential themes of meaning, time, and human existence, combining bleakness with absurd humour.

"Endgame" by Samuel Beckett is another modern tragicomedy in which humour and tragedy intermingle to

reflect on human existence and futility.

Farce: Exaggeration and Humour

Farce is a subgenre of comedy characterised by exaggerated situations, absurd plots, improbable events, and physical humour. It often involves mistaken identities, misunderstandings, and rapid pacing, creating a chaotic and entertaining experience. Farce relies on humour derived from absurdity, exaggeration, and contradiction, often focusing on the ridiculousness of human behaviour.

Characteristics of Farce

Exaggeration: Farce thrives on exaggeration—exaggerated characters, situations, and actions. Characters in a farce often behave in extreme or absurd ways, and situations are pushed to their most ludicrous limits.

Fast Pace: Farces are known for their rapid pacing, which includes quick dialogue, fast-moving action, and a relentless progression of comedic events. This pace keeps the audience engaged and adds to the humour.

Physical Comedy: Farce often relies heavily on physical comedy, such as slapstick, pratfalls, chases, and sight gags. The humour comes from the dialogue and the characters' movements, gestures, and physical interactions.

Improbable Situations: Farce presents highly improbable and exaggerated situations, often involving mistaken identities, hidden motives, and absurd coincidences. These situations create a sense of chaos and unpredictability.

Examples of Farce

"Noises Off" by Michael Frayn: A quintessential example of farce, depicting the chaotic backstage antics of a theatre company. The play features mistaken identities, slapstick humour, and rapid-fire dialogue.

"The Importance of Being Earnest" by Oscar Wilde: While primarily a comedy of manners, Wilde's play incorporates elements of farce through mistaken identities, witty wordplay, and satirical exaggeration.

"The Comedy of Errors" by William Shakespeare: A farce involving two sets of identical twins separated at birth, leading to mistaken identities, misunderstandings, and comic chaos.

Melodrama: Emotion and Action

Melodrama is a type of drama that emphasises emotional appeal, sensationalism, and clear moral distinctions between good and evil. It often features exaggerated characters, intense emotions, and dramatic plots focusing on thrilling action and ethical dilemmas. Melodrama is designed to provoke strong emotional reactions from the audience, often through heightened conflicts and resolutions.

Characteristics of Melodrama

Exaggerated Emotions: Melodramas focus on intense emotional experiences, often portraying characters in extreme distress, danger, or passion. The emotions are heightened to evoke the audience's empathy, sympathy, or outrage.

Clear Moral Polarization: Melodramas typically distinguish between good and evil, hero and villain. Characters are often archetypal or symbolic, representing moral virtues or vices.

Sensational Plot: Melodramatic plots are driven by sensational elements such as betrayal, revenge, love, danger, and injustice. These plots are designed to captivate the audience's attention and keep them on the edge of their seats.

Music and Sound: Music is often used in melodrama to enhance the emotional impact of the scenes, underscoring moments of tension, suspense, or romance.

Evolution of Melodrama

Origins in 19th-Century Theatre: Melodrama emerged as a popular theatrical form in the 19th century, characterised by its use of music, heightened emotion, and moralistic themes. Plays like *"Uncle Tom's Cabin"* and *"East Lynne"* were famous melodramas that addressed social issues of the time.

Adaptations in Film and Television: In the 20th century, melodrama found a new medium in film and television, where its emphasis on emotion and visual spectacle continued to captivate audiences. Classic Hollywood films like *"Gone with the Wind"* and *"Casablanca"* incorporated melodramatic elements.

Examples of Melodrama

"Uncle Tom's Cabin" by Harriet Beecher Stowe: A classic example of 19th-century melodrama that depicts the struggles of enslaved people and the moral issues of slavery.

"The Octoroon" by Dion Boucicault: A melodrama that deals with race, love, and social injustice in the antebellum South, combining sensational plot elements with strong emotional appeal.

"Wuthering Heights" by Emily Brontë (as adapted into stage and screen versions): A melodrama that explores themes of love, revenge, and social conflict in a Gothic setting.

Musical Drama: Storytelling with Music

Musical drama, or musical theatre, is a form of drama that integrates music, songs, dance, and spoken dialogue to tell a story. It combines the elements of drama with the expressive power of music, creating a rich and dynamic theatrical experience. Musical dramas range from lighthearted comedies to profound narratives, often featuring memorable melodies, elaborate choreography, and dynamic performances.

Characteristics of Musical Drama

Integration of Music and Drama: Musical drama blends songs, music, and dance with spoken dialogue and narrative. The music advances the plot, develops characters, and enhances the story's emotional impact.

Choreography: Dance is a critical component of musical drama. It is often used to express emotions, enhance storytelling, and create visual spectacle. Choreography is carefully crafted to complement the music and narrative.

Variety of Genres: Musical dramas encompass various genres, from romantic comedies to historical epics, social commentaries, and adaptations of literary works. They can be severe or lighthearted, traditional or experimental.

Audience Engagement: Musicals are designed to engage the audience through catchy songs, dynamic performances, and immersive staging. They often feature memorable melodies and show-stopping numbers that resonate with audiences.

Examples of Musical Drama

"Les Misérables" by Alain Boublil and Claude-Michel Schönberg: A musical adaptation of Victor Hugo's novel that combines powerful music with a dramatic narrative of love, sacrifice, and redemption during the French Revolution.

"West Side Story" by Leonard Bernstein and Stephen Sondheim: A musical drama that reimagines Shakespeare's *"Romeo and Juliet"* in the context of gang rivalry and forbidden love in 1950s New York.

"Hamilton" by Lin-Manuel Miranda: A modern musical drama that blends hip-hop, R&B, and traditional musical theatre to tell the story of Alexander Hamilton and the founding of the United States.

Documentary Drama: Based on Real Events

Documentary drama, also known as docudrama or verbatim theatre, is a form of drama based on actual events, people, and historical moments. It often uses primary sources, such as interviews, transcripts, letters, and archival material, to create a dramatised representation of reality. Documentary drama aims to educate, inform, and provoke thought by bringing real-life stories and issues to the stage.

Characteristics of Documentary Drama

Authenticity: Documentary dramas strive for authenticity by using actual words, documents, and testimonies to construct the narrative. The dialogue is often taken verbatim from interviews or records, lending a sense of realism and credibility to the performance.

Political and Social Commentary: Many documentary dramas focus on political, social, or historical issues, aiming to raise awareness, provoke debate, and inspire change. They often highlight marginalised voices, expose injustices, or provide alternative perspectives on well-known events.

Minimalist Staging: Documentary dramas often use minimalist staging and simple sets to keep the focus on the content and the real-life events being depicted. The emphasis is on storytelling rather than elaborate visual effects.

Direct Address: Actors in documentary dramas may directly address the audience, breaking the fourth wall to create a sense of immediacy and engagement. This technique helps to draw the audience into the narrative and foster a sense of connection to the real-life events.

Examples of Documentary Drama

"The Laramie Project" by Moisés Kaufman and the Tectonic Theater Project: A documentary drama based on interviews, journal entries, and news reports about the 1998 murder of Matthew Shepard, a gay student in Laramie, Wyoming. The play explores themes of hate, prejudice, and community response.

"My Name is Rachel Corrie" by Alan Rickman and Katharine Viner: A docudrama based on the writings of Rachel Corrie, an American activist who was killed in Gaza while protesting against the Israeli military. The play uses her letters, emails, and diary entries to tell her story.

"Verbatim Theatre": A style of documentary drama that involves the precise recreation of real-life dialogue and events. Examples include *"London Road"* by Alecky Blythe and Adam Cork, which depicts the Ipswich serial murders through interviews with residents.

What We Learnt

In this chapter, we have explored the fundamental components of drama, including plot, character, dialogue, and staging. We have provided a clear framework for analysing various dramatic works by breaking down these elements. We have also examined how drama differs from other literary forms like novels and poems, emphasising its unique reliance on performance and dialogue. This foundational understanding is a stepping stone for a more profound appreciation and critique of dramatic literature.

This knowledge will enable readers to better engage with and analyse dramatic texts as we progress. Recognising the historical shifts and cultural influences on drama helps contextualise and enrich our interpretations.

Whether you're a student, educator, or theatre enthusiast, grasping these core concepts lays the groundwork for a more nuanced appreciation of plays and their performances. With these tools, readers can delve deeper into the intricate world of drama, uncovering the layers of meaning within each work.

CHAPTER II

Ancient Greek Drama

Ancient Greek Drama is the foundation for Western theatrical traditions, blending religious rituals with evolving artistic forms. Emerging from festivals dedicated to Dionysus, these performances integrated worship with societal commentary, creating a unique space for public reflection and dialogue. The transition from choral songs and dances to complex plays marked significant cultural progress. Early Greek drama was pivotal in addressing themes of human experience and divine interaction, enabling society to explore moral and philosophical questions through a structured yet engaging format.

This chapter will delve into the intricate origins and development of Ancient Greek Drama. It discusses the role of religion in shaping early performances and traces the evolution of dramatic techniques over time. Readers will gain insights into critical figures like Aeschylus, Sophocles, and Euripides, whose contributions significantly advanced the art form. The chapter also examines the structure of Greek tragedies, including their typical elements, themes, and dramatic techniques. Finally, it explores how political and social changes influenced Greek drama, highlighting its lasting legacy and continued relevance in modern theatre and literature.

Origins and Development

Ancient Greek Drama emerged as one of Western culture's most influential forms of artistic expression. Its origins can be traced back to the interplay between religion and theatre in Ancient Greece, where dramatic performances were initially part of religious festivals. These performances served as acts of worship and as a form of societal commentary.

In terms of cultural context, Ancient Greek drama was closely linked to the worship of Dionysus, the god of wine, fertility, and revelry. The City Dionysia festival in Athens featured dramatic competitions and was integral to the social and religious calendar. The theatre explored human experiences and divine interactions, addressing themes like fate, morality, and the human condition. This intertwining of religion and theatre created a unique space for reflection and dialogue within Greek society.

Early Greek drama evolved from purely religious rituals to more structured dramatic performances as the art form evolved. Initially, these performances consisted of choral songs and dances performed in honour of Dionysus. Over time, they developed into more complex plays with distinct genres like tragedy and comedy. Tragedy, characterised by its sombre themes and severe tone, often deals with profound moral and philosophical questions, exploring the consequences of human actions and the inevitability of fate. Comedy, on the other hand, provided a satirical take on contemporary society, poking fun at political leaders, social norms, and everyday life.

The contributions of the chorus played a pivotal role in this transformation. In early Greek drama, the chorus consisted of performers who sang, danced, and interacted with the main characters. They served as a narrative device, providing background information, summarising events, and reflecting on the moral implications of the story. The chorus was also seen as the voice of societal values, offering commentary on the action and guiding the audience's interpretation of the play. Their presence helped bridge the gap between the actors and the audience, creating a communal experience emphasising shared values and collective reflection.

Several historical milestones marked the development of Greek drama. One significant transition was the introduction of individual actors. Thespis considered the first actor, stepped out of the chorus to deliver lines, making dialogues possible and adding complexity to the narrative. This innovation laid the groundwork for future developments in playwriting and performance. Another milestone was the establishment of playwriting competitions during festivals like the City Dionysia. These competitions fostered creativity and innovation as playwrights vied for recognition and prestige. The competitive atmosphere led to the refinement of dramatic techniques and the emergence of notable playwrights who contributed to the art form's evolution.

Political influences also shaped the trajectory of Greek drama. Athens, a prominent city-state, experienced significant political and social changes during the 5th century BCE. The rise of democracy brought new perspectives and ideas, which were reflected in the plays of the time. Dramatists used their works to comment on political issues, question authority, and engage in debates about civic responsibility. This integration of politics and theatre underscored the importance of drama as a platform for public discourse and engagement.

Key Playwrights: Aeschylus, Sophocles, Euripides

Ancient Greek drama owes much of its foundational strength and enduring influence to the contributions of three key playwrights: Aeschylus, Sophocles, and Euripides. Each brought unique innovations and themes that profoundly shaped the genre, leaving a lasting legacy on Western dramatic traditions.

Aeschylus is often hailed as the father of tragedy. His work marked a significant departure from previous forms of storytelling by introducing the second actor on stage. This innovation allowed for dynamic interactions between characters and added depth to the narrative structure of Greek plays. Before Aeschylus, dramas were primarily driven by the chorus, which narrated events and provided moral commentary. Including an additional actor enabled the exploration of intricate human relationships and conflicts, pushing the boundaries of what drama could achieve.

Aeschylus also delved into themes such as fate and divine justice. In his trilogy, "The Oresteia," he explores the cycle of vengeance within a family and the eventual establishment of legal justice over personal retribution. Through these themes, Aeschylus pondered on the role of the gods in human affairs and the inevitability of destiny. His works underscored the tension between individual actions and overarching divine will, prompting audiences to reflect on their lives and choices within the broader cosmic order.

Sophocles, another pivotal figure in Greek drama, built upon the innovations of Aeschylus by introducing the third actor. This further expanded the potential for complex interactions among characters, elevating the dramatic experience. Sophocles focused on character development and moral complexity, presenting protagonists who were relatable yet flawed. His tragedies often centred on the concept of tragic flaws, where characters‘ inherent weaknesses led them to their downfall.

One of the most notable examples is "Oedipus Rex." The protagonist, Oedipus, is depicted as a noble and determined leader whose tragic flaw—his hubris and determination to defy prophecy—ultimately leads to his ruin. Sophocles masterfully employed irony and dramatic tension to heighten the story's emotional impact, making the audience acutely aware of the impending disaster while watching the characters grapple with their fate. This use of dramatic irony not only deepened the emotional resonance of his plays but also invited the audience to question the nature of fate and free will.

Euripides, considered the most modern of the three, introduced a distinct approach to Greek drama by challenging societal norms and emphasising individual psychology. His plays often featured complex female characters and explored themes of human emotion and social critique. Euripides was less focused on the divine than his predecessors and more interested in portraying realistic human experiences and motivations.

In Medea, Euripides powerfully depicts a woman scorned by her husband and driven to extreme measures out of anger and betrayal. Medea's character is multifaceted, evoking both sympathy and horror from the audience. Euripides' focus on psychological depth and emotional authenticity made his characters and narratives more relatable, setting the stage for future explorations of individual experiences in drama.

The legacy of Aeschylus, Sophocles, and Euripides extends far beyond their lifetime. Their contributions laid the groundwork for many dramatic conventions and archetypes that persist in theatre today. For instance, the innovative use of multiple actors and complex character interactions set a precedent for narrative depth that influenced later playwrights, including Shakespeare. Themes like fate, justice, and individual agency, first explored by these Greek dramatists, continue to resonate in contemporary literature and film.

Furthermore, these playwrights‘ structural elements and character archetypes have become foundational components of Western theatrical tradition. The tragic hero, marked by a fatal flaw, remains a central figure in modern narratives, demonstrating the enduring power of Greek drama's influence. The moral dilemmas and ethical questions posed by Aeschylus, Sophocles, and Euripides invite continuous reflection and reinterpretation, bridging the gap between ancient and modern times.

Structure of Greek Tragedy

Defining Greek Tragedy: Formal Elements and Techniques

The formal elements of Greek tragedy are central to understanding its impact on Western drama. The structured nature of these plays was pivotal in conveying their themes and engaging audiences. This subpoint delves into the typical structure, recurring themes and motifs, dramatic techniques, and the interplay of structure and story in Greek tragedies.

Typical Structure

Greek tragedies followed a highly defined structure that helped shape the narrative and engage the audience through stages. The play typically begins with a prologue, an introductory section where one or more characters set the scene and provide background information for understanding the forthcoming action. This was followed by the parodos, the entrance song of the chorus, which often contained further exposition and set the emotional tone of the play.

Next came the episodes, which were scenes where the main action unfolded. Characters interacted, conflicts arose, and the plot progressed. Between these episodes, the chorus would perform stasimon, choral odes that reflected on the events, offered philosophical insights, or foreshadowed future developments. These interludes allowed the audience to digest the preceding action and added depth to the narrative.

The play concludes with the departure, the final scene in which the resolution occurs. Here, the consequences of the protagonist's actions are revealed, and any remaining questions are addressed. This structure provides a clear storytelling framework and allows playwrights to manipulate tension and pacing effectively.

Themes and Motifs

Central to Greek tragedy were themes like fate, choice, and morality. These themes were interwoven into the narratives, influencing the characters' actions and the play's overall message. Fate often played a dominant role, depicted as an unavoidable force that characters could not escape, no matter how hard they tried. This is seen in works such as Sophocles' "Oedipus Rex," where Oedipus cannot escape his prophesied fate despite his efforts to avoid it.

Choice and free will were equally significant, presenting characters with moral dilemmas that tested their virtues and flaws. The tension between fate and free will created a complex dynamic, as characters had to navigate their paths amidst predetermined outcomes. Morality, another key motif, explored the ethical dimensions of human actions, often highlighting the consequences of hubris, pride, and defiance against divine order.

Dramatic Techniques

To enhance these themes, Greek tragedians employed various dramatic techniques. Dramatic irony was a prevalent tool, where the audience knew more about the true circumstances than the characters. This technique heightened emotional engagement as viewers anticipated the inevitable consequences that the characters were oblivious to. For example, in "Oedipus Rex," the audience knows from the beginning that Oedipus himself is the murderer he seeks, intensifying the tragic impact of his discovery.

Foreshadowing was another common technique, providing subtle hints or outright predictions about future events. This kept the audience intrigued and maintained suspense throughout the play. By offering glimpses of what was to come, playwrights could build anticipation and deepen the emotional resonance of the unfolding drama.

Suspense development was intricately linked with the structure and character interactions. Through well-paced episodes and strategic placement of choral odes, playwrights controlled the rhythm of the narrative, escalating tension at critical moments. The interplay between dialogue and choral reflection allowed audiences to experience a rollercoaster of emotions, from anxiety to catharsis.

Interplay of Structure and Story

The structured nature of Greek tragedy directly influenced character development and plot progression.

The prologue laid the groundwork, introducing characters and their initial motivations. As the episodes unfolded, protagonists faced escalating challenges that tested their morals and decisions. This episodic progression mirrored the characters' journeys, allowing for gradual but significant development.

Moral dilemmas were central to this development. Protagonists often found themselves at a crossroads where they had to choose between conflicting values. Their choices revealed their true nature and determined their ultimate fate. For instance, in Euripides‘ "Medea," Medea's decision to avenge her husband's betrayal highlights her resolve and complexity as a character, even as it leads to tragic consequences.

The stasimon provided moments of reflection, where the chorus contemplated the ethical implications of the characters' actions. This added philosophical depth and invited the audience to reflect on the moral issues presented. The structure reinforced the thematic explorations of fate, choice, and morality by juxtaposing action with contemplation.

Influence on Later Forms of Drama

Ancient Greek drama has left an indelible mark on Western theatrical traditions, and its influence can be traced through various historical periods, particularly in European theatrical traditions during the Renaissance and beyond. The cultural relevance of Greek drama is evident in how it laid the foundational elements for later theatrical forms, often serving as a template for storytelling and performance techniques. The Renaissance period, for instance, witnessed a revival of classical texts, including

Greek dramas, which were translated, adapted, and staged across Europe. Playwrights like William Shakespeare drew heavily from Greek conventions, incorporating aspects such as the tragic hero and chorus-like commentary through characters.

Adapting techniques from Greek drama is another critical factor in understanding its lasting influence. Greek playwrights such as Aeschylus, Sophocles, and Euripides developed dramatic techniques that have become essential elements of modern playwriting. One of these techniques is dramatic irony, where the audience is aware of critical information unknown to the characters. This method heightens tension and engagement, a practice in many modern plays and films. The tragic flaw, or "hamartia," introduced by Aristotle in his analysis of Greek tragedies, remains a pivotal element in character development within contemporary drama. These ancient techniques continue to shape narrative structures and character arcs in modern storytelling.

Greek drama did more than entertain; it provided a platform for cultural critique, exploring moral, ethical, and social issues that resonate even in today's world. The themes in Greek dramas, such as justice, power, fate, and the human condition, are timeless and universal. Plays like Sophocles' "Antigone" delve into conflicts between individual rights and state laws, a theme still relevant in contemporary governance and civil disobedience discussions. Similarly, Euripides' "Medea" examines the complexities of revenge and the plight of women in a patriarchal society, offering insights that continue to provoke thought and discussion in modern contexts. By addressing such enduring themes, Greek drama transcends its historical origins, speaking to generations across time.

The ongoing impact of Greek drama is also evident in its presence across various forms of modern media, including film, literature, and theatre. Many contemporary works draw inspiration from Greek mythology and drama, reinterpreting ancient stories to reflect current societal norms and values. For instance, films like "O Brother, Where Art Thou?" by the Coen Brothers pay homage to Homer's "Odyssey," showcasing the adaptability and relevance of Greek narratives. Additionally, numerous theatrical productions continue to stage ancient Greek plays, sometimes with modernised settings or interpretations, highlighting their continuing appeal and significance. The structural elements of Greek tragedy, with its clear beginning, climax, and resolution, offer a blueprint that continues to inform the construction of modern narratives.

Contributions and Lasting Legacy

Ancient Greek Drama has profoundly impacted the development of Western theatrical traditions, leaving an enduring legacy. The foundational elements of Ancient Greek drama were heavily influenced by religious and societal contexts, particularly the festivals held in honour of the god Dionysus. These festivals often included performances that eventually evolved into formalised dramatic presentations. The rituals and community gatherings provided fertile ground for the emergence of theatre, linking it closely with both worship and social commentary.

As drama evolved, key playwrights such as Aeschylus, Sophocles, and Euripides introduced innovations that significantly advanced dramatic techniques and storytelling. Aeschylus is often credited with adding a second actor to plays, enabling dialogue and more complex interactions between characters. This innovation was crucial in transforming simple narratives into intricate plots involving themes of fate and divine justice. Sophocles, another prominent figure, brought further refinement by introducing a third actor and enhancing character development and moral complexity. His approach allowed for deeper emotional resonance and exploration of human flaws through tragic irony. Euripides, known for his modern sensibilities, challenged societal norms by focusing on individual psychology and portraying complex female characters, thus deepening the narrative richness of drama.

The structure of Greek tragedy also played a monumental role in shaping Western theatrical forms. Traditional Greek tragedy followed a specific structure consisting of the prologue, parodos, episodes, stasimon, and exodus. This framework provided a clear story progression and facilitated the development of dramatic tension and resolution. The emphasis on structured acts and choruses influenced later theatrical genres, laying the groundwork for narrative coherence and emotional pacing in modern drama.

Greek dramas frequently dealt with universal themes such as fate, choice, and morality, which continue to resonate today. The narratives explored profound moral and ethical dilemmas, often invoking catharsis—a term coined by Aristotle to describe the emotional purging experienced by the audience. This focus on universal human experiences gives ancient Greek drama a timeless quality, allowing contemporary audiences to connect deeply with the stories despite the historical distance.

The structural elements of Greek drama also included the chorus, a group of performers who commented on the action and interacted with the main characters. The chorus served multiple functions: it provided background information, reflected public opinion, and allowed for thematic commentary, enriching the narrative depth. This inclusion significantly influenced subsequent theatrical traditions, where similar devices have provided exposition and deepened audience engagement.

The influence of Ancient Greek themes and structures is evident in modern drama. Contemporary playwrights and filmmakers draw inspiration from Greek tragedies when crafting their narratives. The exploration of tragic flaws, moral complexities, and psychological depth continues to captivate audiences. For instance, modern adaptations of classical myths or reinterpretations of ancient plays are common in today's theatre, showcasing the enduring relevance of these ancient themes.

Moreover, Greek drama's exploration of societal and individual conflicts remains pertinent. Issues like power dynamics, gender roles, and ethical choices portrayed in ancient texts are mirrored in contemporary narratives, highlighting ongoing societal concerns. By revisiting these themes, modern creators can address current issues while paying homage to the origins of Western drama.

The lasting contributions of Ancient Greek drama extend beyond the realm of theatre into various aspects of culture and education. Studying Greek plays is integral to understanding the evolution of literature and drama, offering valuable insights into narrative techniques, character development, and thematic exploration. Educators use these classical texts to illustrate fundamental concepts in storytelling and dramatic arts, ensuring that the legacy of Ancient Greek drama endures in academic settings.

The societal impact of Greek drama also reveals its enduring legacy. Public performances of these plays still occur, often in outdoor theatres reminiscent of ancient times. These performances celebrate cultural heritage and unite communities like the original festivals honouring Dionysus. This communal aspect underscores the significance of theatre in fostering social cohesion and collective reflection.

What We Learnt

The chapter explored the origins and development of Ancient Greek drama, illustrating its profound connection to religious festivals dedicated to Dionysus, which served as worship and societal commentary. The evolution from choral songs and dances to structured dramatic performances, including tragedy and comedy, highlighted how themes of fate, morality, and human experiences were woven into these plays. Key historical milestones, such as introducing individual actors and playwriting competitions, were pivotal in advancing dramatic techniques and fostering creativity among playwrights.

Additionally, the contributions of seminal playwrights Aeschylus, Sophocles, and Euripides have been examined, each bringing unique innovations that shaped the genre's complexity and depth. Their works delved into themes of fate, divine justice, and individual psychology, setting precedents for character development and narrative structure still relevant today. The influence of Greek drama extends beyond its time, impacting later forms of drama and continuing to resonate through its exploration of universal human themes, offering valuable insights for students, educators, and theatre enthusiasts alike.

CHAPTER III

Medieval and Renaissance Drama

Medieval and Renaissance drama represents a significant evolution in theatrical forms, marked by a transition from morality plays to Shakespearean masterpieces. This period showcases the transformative journey of drama, reflecting broader cultural and intellectual shifts that influenced storytelling and performance techniques. By exploring the foundations laid during the Medieval period and their development through the Renaissance, the chapter highlights how early dramatic traditions evolved to create more complex and multifaceted works of literature.

In this chapter, readers will delve into the characteristics of Medieval drama, focusing on its emphasis on biblical stories, the use of pageant wagons, and the inclusion of vernacular languages to engage diverse audiences. These plays‘ educational and moral functions and the communal aspects that brought local communities together will be examined. Moving forward, the chapter will address the significance of morality and mystery plays, detailing their role in medieval society and their impact on audience engagement. Finally, the chapter will trace the progression to Renaissance drama, with particular attention given to the influence of Humanism, the revival of classical Greek and Roman traditions, and the profound contributions of playwrights like William Shakespeare. Through this exploration, readers will gain a deeper understanding of the critical characteristics, pivotal forms, and lasting impact of both Medieval and Renaissance drama.

Characteristics of Medieval Drama

Medieval drama played a crucial role in shaping the future of theatrical forms by incorporating unique elements that resonated deeply with audiences. One of the most defining aspects of medieval drama was its focus on biblical stories. These plays often depicted scenes from the Bible, bringing to life the narratives central to the Christian faith. By dramatising these religious stories, medieval dramas helped audiences connect more profoundly with their faith. Portraying moral and spiritual dilemmas allowed spectators to reflect on their beliefs and ethics tangibly.

Moreover, medieval drama utilised distinct performative formats, among which pageant wagons were especially notable. These mobile stages allowed performances to travel from one location to another, reaching diverse communities. This mobility meant that dramatic performances were not confined to a single location or specific audience but could engage with various social groups across different regions. Pageant wagons enabled performances in public spaces, making theatre an accessible and communal event. The ability to transport these elaborate stages also demonstrated the resourcefulness and ingenuity of medieval performers and set designers.

Another significant feature of medieval drama was using vernacular languages instead of Latin, commonly used in religious and scholarly contexts. By employing local dialects and languages, these plays became more accessible to the general population. This accessibility significantly increased drama's popularity and cultural significance during this period. People who might not have understood

Latin could now follow and enjoy the performances, enhancing their engagement and comprehension. Integrating vernacular languages into theatrical performances also contributed to developing national literature and cultures, fostering a sense of identity and unity among audiences.

The teaching function of medieval drama cannot be understated. These plays were designed not only to entertain but also to educate. Their narratives conveyed important social and spiritual ethics, encouraging audiences to contemplate their morals and behaviours. For example, characters often face moral choices highlighting virtues such as honesty, compassion, and selflessness and vices like greed, envy, and deceit. By witnessing the consequences of these choices, audiences were prompted to reflect on their actions and consider the ethical implications of their decisions.

Medieval drama often incorporated figurative elements, where characters personified abstract concepts such as Good Deeds, Knowledge, and Death. These allegories made complex spiritual and moral teachings more relatable and understandable to the audience. Personification allowed for a more precise depiction of moral lessons, illustrating the internal struggle between good and evil in an engaging and instructive manner. This method of storytelling ensured that the lessons imparted by the plays remained memorable and impactful.

The communal aspect of medieval drama was further emphasised through the involvement of local communities in the production and performance of these plays. Townspeople often participated as actors, stagehands, and organisers, fostering a strong sense of community and collaboration. This collective effort brought people together and strengthened social bonds and communal identities. The shared experience of creating and watching these performances reinforced the values and beliefs central to the community's way of life.

In addition to moral and spiritual instruction, medieval drama also provided entertainment and escapism for audiences. The colourful costumes, elaborate sets, and dramatic storylines captivated viewers, offering them a reprieve from the hardships of daily life. These plays' blend of humour, tragedy, and suspense ensured they were educational and enjoyable to watch. This balance of instruction and entertainment helped secure the enduring appeal of medieval drama and laid the groundwork for future theatrical forms.

The legacy of medieval drama is evident in its influence on subsequent theatrical traditions. The emphasis on moral and ethical reflection carried over into later periods, including the Renaissance, where themes of human struggle and virtue continued to be explored. Using vernacular languages paved the way for the flourishing of national literature and the rise of playwrights who wrote in their native tongues. The performative formats developed during the medieval period also evolved, leading to more sophisticated staging techniques and theatre designs in the following centuries.

Furthermore, medieval drama's communal nature—wherein entire communities would come together to produce and perform plays—can be seen as a precursor to modern-day theatre ensembles and community theatre groups. This collaborative spirit continues to thrive in contemporary theatre, highlighting the enduring impact of medieval drama on the arts.

Morality and Mystery Plays

Medieval and Renaissance drama saw a significant evolution from morality and mystery plays to Shakespearean masterpieces, reflecting the transformative journey of drama during these periods. We can better understand this transition by exploring how morality and mystery plays served educational and narrative functions in medieval society.

Morality plays were a distinctive form of drama that emerged in medieval Europe around the 15th century. These plays depicted the human struggle between virtues and vices, making ethical dilemmas relatable to the audience. Characters often personified moral attributes like Good Deeds, Knowledge, and Vice, providing a clear moral message. For example, one of the most famous morality plays, *Everyman*, centres on the titular character's journey to death and his reckoning with his life's choices. Everyman illustrated the importance of living a virtuous life through its symbolic characters and straightforward narrative. The play's accessibility helped audiences, regardless of their literacy levels, engage with its themes and reflect on their moral choices.

On the other hand, mystery plays focused primarily on biblical stories and events, effectively engaging audiences with their religious beliefs. These plays were often performed during religious festivals like the Feast of Corpus Christi, blending entertainment with spiritual education. Mystery plays were structured as cycles, which meant they included a series of short plays that together told a comprehensive narrative from Creation to Judgment Day. One well-known cycle is the York Mystery Plays, which covered vital biblical events such as the Creation, the Fall of Man, the Passion, and the Resurrection. These dramatisations enabled audiences to understand their faith better, bringing scripture to life vividly and memorably. The visual and performative elements made abstract biblical stories more tangible and impactful.

Audience participation was another critical element of morality and mystery plays, forming a sense of belonging and investment in the narrative experience. The medieval drama was not confined to the stage; it often spilt over into the audience, inviting them to become part of the story. This interaction created a communal atmosphere where the viewers felt intricately connected to the narrative. For instance, scenes requiring audience responses or interactive moments where actors moved through the crowd dissolved the boundary between performers and spectators. This engagement fostered a shared experience, allowing people to feel directly involved in the portrayed moral and spiritual lessons. Such involvement increased the emotional resonance of the plays and ensured the audience more deeply internalised the messages.

Exploring these human experiences in medieval drama set the stage for more profound character studies in Renaissance drama. By focusing on the intricate dynamics of human virtues and vices and the profound impact of biblical narratives, these early forms of drama paved the way for more complex character development and storytelling—Renaissance playwrights, including William Shakespeare, built upon this foundation, creating multifaceted characters with psychological depth. The complexity of Shakespeare's characters, such as Hamlet's existential angst or Lady Macbeth's ambitious guilt, can be traced back to the moral deliberations seen in medieval plays.

Moreover, the narrative techniques and audience engagement strategies in morality and mystery plays influenced how Renaissance dramas were structured and performed. The emphasis on relatable ethical and spiritual themes transitioned into nuanced explorations of human nature, personal ambition, and societal issues. Themes from medieval drama, like the battle between good and evil or the consequences of one's actions, evolved into sophisticated plots that still resonate with modern audiences.

Introduction to Renaissance Drama

Emergence and Distinctive Features of Renaissance Drama

The emergence of Renaissance drama marked a fundamental shift in theatrical history, reflecting broader European cultural revolutions during the 14th to 17th centuries. A pivotal influence on this evolution was the rise of Humanism, a movement that significantly emphasised human potential, individual experience, and complex character development. This intellectual revival encouraged playwrights to explore deeper psychological dimensions within their characters. Unlike Medieval dramaturgy, which often portrayed stereotypical representations of virtues and vices, Renaissance drama embraced multifaceted characters who grappled with internal conflicts and moral ambiguities, mirroring the complexities of human nature.

Humanism's impact on drama is evident in the works of prominent playwrights like Christopher Marlowe and William Shakespeare, whose characters exhibit profound depth and personal struggles. For instance, Marlowe's "Doctor Faustus" delves into Faustus' inner turmoil as he oscillates between ambition and repentance, illuminating the Renaissance fascination with human potential and existential dilemmas. Similarly, Shakespeare's Hamlet is a paragon of human complexity; his psyche is laid bare through soliloquies that reveal his introspective nature and vacillation between action and inaction.

Another cornerstone of Renaissance drama was the revival of classical Greek and Roman literary traditions. Playwrights drew inspiration from ancient texts, adopting and adapting classical plot structures, themes, and stylistic elements to enrich their narratives. The rediscovery of Aristotle's works on tragedy and Horace's on poetics provided a theoretical foundation that informed dramatic compositions. This classical resurgence fostered new storytelling approaches that departed from the didactic and religious focus of Medieval plays, instead celebrating secular themes and the human condition.

The revival of classical forms also introduced the concept of the three unities—unity of time, place, and action—principles derived from Aristotle's "Poetics." Although not rigidly adhered to by all playwrights, these unities influenced the construction of coherent, focused narratives, contributing to the overall aesthetic quality of theatre. This period saw a harmonious blend of classical motifs with contemporary ideas, resulting in innovative and dynamic dramatic works.

The establishment of professional theatres was another transformative factor in Renaissance drama. Before this era, theatrical performances were confined mainly to church-sponsored events or itinerant troupes performing in makeshift venues. However, constructing permanent playhouses, such as The Globe and The Rose in London, revolutionised the theatrical landscape. These venues enabled regular performances, attracted diverse audiences, and significantly expanded the scope for artistic experimentation.

Professional theatres democratised the theatergoing experience by making it accessible to a broader population segment, including nobility and commoners. This inclusivity fostered a vibrant theatrical culture where various stories could be told, appealing to multiple tastes and social strata. Additionally, the physical structure of these theatres, with their thrust stages and open galleries, created an intimate atmosphere that enhanced audience engagement and interaction with the performers.

The development of new genres further contributed to the richness of Renaissance drama. Tragedy, comedy, and history became distinct categories with conventions and thematic concerns. Tragedies during this period delved into profound themes of fate, ambition, and human suffering, often drawing on classical influences. For example, Shakespeare's "Macbeth" explores the tragic consequences of unchecked ambition, while "Othello" examines the destructive power of jealousy and mistrust.

On the other hand, comedies celebrated the lighter aspects of human experience, often employing wit, humour, and satire to critique social norms and human follies. Ben Jonson's "Volpone" exemplifies this genre, using comedic elements to expose greed and corruption in society. Shakespearean comedies like "A Midsummer Night's Dream" and "Twelfth Night" presented intricate plots woven with mistaken identities, romantic entanglements, and playful misunderstandings, ultimately resolving in harmony and reconciliation.

Historical dramas emerged as a genre that dramatised historical events and figures, offering audiences a theatrical window into the past. These plays blended factual history with imaginative storytelling, creating compelling narratives that reflected contemporary concerns through historical lenses. Shakespeare's history plays, such as "Henry V" and "Richard III," are notable for their exploration of political power, leadership, and national identity, resonating with audiences both then and now.

In summary, Renaissance drama was characterised by several definitive features that distinguished it from its Medieval predecessor. Influenced by Humanism, it emphasised human potential and complex character development, portraying individuals with rich psychological depth. The revival of classical Greek and Roman works infused new storytelling approaches, enriching narratives with timeless themes and structures. The emergence of professional theatres democratised the theatre experience, allowing for more diverse and dynamic performances. Lastly, the development of new genres, including tragedy, comedy, and history, led to more vibrant storytelling, cementing the profound impact of Renaissance drama on the trajectory of theatrical history.

Impact of William Shakespeare

William Shakespeare's contributions to drama represent a monumental shift in the landscape of theatrical art during the Renaissance. His works not only set new standards but also encapsulated the essence of this transformative period.

Shakespeare's characters are renowned for their depth and internal conflicts, which have significantly elevated dramatic narrative standards. Unlike earlier dramatic characters who were often one-dimensional, Shakespeare introduced multi-faceted individuals struggling with complex emotions and ethical dilemmas. For instance, Hamlet's existential quandaries or Lady Macbeth's consuming ambition offer audiences rich psychological portraits that invite deeper analysis. This complexity allows actors to explore various dimensions within a single role, making performances more engaging and relatable.

His innovative use of language also played a crucial role in enriching the dramatic experience. Shakespeare's mastery of metaphor and wordplay is evident throughout his plays. Terms like "the world is my oyster" from *The Merry Wives of Windsor* or "brevity is the soul of wit" from *Hamlet* have become part of the everyday lexicon, demonstrating his linguistic influence. Such inventive language not only adds layers of meaning but also enhances the emotional impact of the dialogue. The soliloquies in his plays, particularly in *Hamlet* and *Macbeth*, showcase his unparalleled ability to delve into the human psyche using poetic devices. These elements collectively make his work timelessly appealing and intellectually stimulating.

Another cornerstone of Shakespeare's work is his exploration of universal themes. He delves into love, power, guilt, and fate—topics that resonate across different eras and cultures. Plays like *Romeo and Juliet* explore the tragic consequences of young love and familial conflict, while *Macbeth* tackles the corrupting influence of power and unchecked ambition. Shakespeare offers insights into human nature that remain relevant today through these narratives. His portrayal of guilt and redemption in *Othello* and *King Lear* continues to influence modern storytelling by providing templates for character arcs and moral questioning.

Shakespeare's lasting impact extends beyond literature into psychology and popular culture. His nuanced characters and intricate plots have informed psychological studies, contributing to our understanding of human behaviour and development. Concepts like the "Oedipal Complex" have drawn inspiration from his characters' relationships, illustrating his reach beyond the realm of drama. Furthermore, his works have been adapted countless times in various formats, from film and television to graphic novels and video games, cementing his role in shaping contemporary culture. Modern adaptations such as Baz Luhrmann's *Romeo + Juliet* and Kenneth Branagh's *Hamlet* bring Shakespeare's stories to new audiences, proving his work's enduring appeal and versatility.

Moreover, Shakespeare's influence can be seen in educational curriculums worldwide, where his plays serve as fundamental texts for studying English literature and drama. Educators utilise his works to teach literary devices, historical context, and critical thinking skills, highlighting their pedagogical value. By analysing his plays, students gain a deeper appreciation for narrative structure and thematic development, essential academic and personal growth tools.

In the theatre world, Shakespeare's contributions continue to inform performance techniques and stagecraft. His plays demand high skill and versatility from actors, who must navigate the intricate language and layered characterisations. Training programs often use his works to hone actors' abilities in voice modulation, emotional expression, and physical movement. Additionally, his enduring popularity ensures that professional theatres frequently stage his plays, keeping his legacy alive and accessible to contemporary audiences.

Legacy of Medieval and Renaissance Drama

The enduring influence of medieval and Renaissance drama on contemporary theatre cannot be overstated. These periods laid the groundwork for many dramatic techniques, structures, and themes still prevalent in modern theatrical works. We can better appreciate their lasting impact by examining specific characteristics and innovations from these eras.

Medieval drama introduced several foundational elements that significantly influenced later forms of theatre. This period is known for its morality plays, which embodied allegorical tales in which characters personified moral attributes such as virtue and vice. These plays provided audiences with clear ethical lessons and mirrored the social norms and concerns of the time. Mystery plays, often staged during religious festivals, depicted biblical events and stories. Both types fostered a communal atmosphere as entire towns participated in performances as actors or spectators, thus integrating theatre into everyday life.

The evolution of audience interaction during this period is particularly noteworthy. Medieval drama encouraged active engagement through interactive storytelling and communal participation. Morality plays presented moral dilemmas that resonated deeply with viewers' personal experiences, promoting introspection and discussion. Mystery plays' captivating enactment of familiar biblical narratives drew large crowds and spurred a shared cultural and religious experience. The community fostered by these performances helped solidify theatre as an important social activity, an attribute that persists in various forms today.

Moving into the Renaissance, a significant shift was influenced by humanism and a revival of classical forms. Humanism emphasises individual potential and complex character development, steering drama from purely didactic purposes toward more nuanced human nature and emotional explorations. Playwrights like Christopher Marlowe and Ben Jonson started creating characters with intricate psychological profiles and realistic motivations. This focus on depth and personality made a heightened relatability, allowing audiences to see fragments of themselves within the characters' struggles and triumphs.

Furthermore, the Renaissance also heralded a revival of classical Greek and Roman plays, introducing new storytelling methods and genres to the stage. These classical influences brought back a structured approach to plot development, including clear distinctions between genres such as tragedy and comedy. The fusion of classical structure with humanistic content enriched the narrative complexity of the period's dramas, making them layered and multifaceted. This era set a precedent for character-driven plots and sophisticated thematic exploration, both of which remain central to contemporary theatre.

Shakespeare, arguably the most eminent figure of the Renaissance drama, encapsulated the spirit of this transformative period. His contributions to the field are monumental, influencing countless aspects of modern storytelling and drama. Shakespeare's characters are renowned for their psychological depth and internal conflicts, differing from the more straightforward characterisations in earlier medieval plays. Figures like Hamlet, Macbeth, and Lear grapple with substantial existential and moral questions, adding complexity to their narratives.

Moreover, Shakespeare's innovative use of language, including his masterful deployment of metaphor, wordplay, and iambic pentameter, enriched the dramatic experience and expanded the expressive potential of the English language itself. His ability to blend poetic devices with authentic dialogue has inspired generations of playwrights and poets. The themes he explored, such as love, power, betrayal, and fate, transcend the specifics of time and place, lending his work a timeless quality that resonates with audiences today.

Shakespeare also set high artistic standards for future generations, shaping subsequent playwrights' and actors' expectations and aspirations. Modern theatre frequently draws upon his works for inspiration, whether through direct adaptations or by integrating elements of his storytelling techniques. Productions of Shakespearean plays are a staple in contemporary theatre repertoires worldwide, demonstrating their enduring relevance and appeal.

What We Learnt

The chapter explored the evolution of drama from medieval morality and mystery plays to the sophisticated works of the Renaissance, particularly those of William Shakespeare. We delved into how medieval drama's focus on biblical stories and moral lessons laid the groundwork for later theatre developments. The unique performative formats, like pageant wagons and vernacular languages, made these plays accessible and engaging for a broad audience. Additionally, the communal aspect of these performances fostered social bonds and reinforced shared values within communities.

Transitioning into Renaissance drama, the chapter highlighted how the rise of humanism brought a new emphasis on individual potential and complex character development. This period saw the revival of classical Greek and Roman literary traditions, influencing plot structures and thematic diversity. William Shakespeare emerged as a seminal figure, with his characters displaying profound psychological depth and ethical dilemmas. His innovative use of language and exploration of universal themes ensured his impact on contemporary and future dramatic works. The transformative journey from medieval to Renaissance drama showcases these periods' enduring legacy and profound influence on modern theatre.

CHAPTER IV

Modern Drama

Modern drama represents a significant evolution in the theatrical landscape, characterised by its departure from classical forms and its embrace of realism and naturalism. This transformation reflects a broader cultural shift towards depicting authentic human experiences and societal issues, moving away from the idealised and mythical narratives that dominated earlier dramatic works. The emergence of modern drama marked by the pursuit of authenticity has profoundly influenced both playwrights' craft and audiences' expectations, fundamentally altering the approach to storytelling on stage.

This chapter will explore the transition from classical drama to modern realism and naturalism, highlighting fundamental movements and figures shaping contemporary theatre. We will examine how realism emerged as a reaction to the exaggerated representations of classical drama, focusing on the authenticity and complexity of ordinary life. The works of pivotal playwrights such as Henrik Ibsen and Anton Chekhov will be discussed, illustrating how their plays tackled pressing social issues and introduced multidimensional characters. Furthermore, we will delve into naturalism's scientific approach, which emphasises the influence of environment and heredity on human behaviour and how it contributed to a deeper understanding of character motivations. Through these explorations, readers will gain insight into the developments that have made modern drama a powerful medium for social commentary and artistic expression.

Realism and Naturalism in Drama

The transition from classical forms of drama to realism and naturalism marked a pivotal shift in the theatre landscape, leading to more authentic and relatable depictions of everyday life and societal issues. This evolution in dramatic style has had profound implications for both playwrights and audiences, fundamentally altering expectations and approaches to storytelling on stage.

Realism emerged as a reaction against classical drama's often grandiose and idealised representations. It sought to portray ordinary life with all its complexities, focusing on the experiences and struggles of ordinary people rather than those of nobility or mythic heroes. Realist plays emphasise authenticity, aiming to mirror reality as closely as possible. Characters were crafted to resemble actual human beings, complete with flaws and contradictions, engaging in dialogue that reflected actual speech patterns rather than heightened or poetic language. This move towards authenticity provided audiences with stories they could see themselves in and issues that resonated with their lives, making theatre a powerful medium for social commentary.

One of the principal aims of realism was to highlight societal issues pertinent to the time, ranging from class struggles and economic hardships to the roles of women and family dynamics. Playwrights such as Henrik Ibsen and Anton Chekhov became prominent figures in this movement, utilising their works to delve into these themes deeply. For instance, Ibsen's "A Doll's House" scrutinises the constraints placed upon women within a patriarchal society, challenging traditional gender roles and sparking discourse on women's rights. By grounding their narratives in real societal contexts, realist plays fostered a greater awareness among audiences about the pressing issues of their day.

In parallel with realism, naturalism took a step further by incorporating scientific principles to examine human behaviour. Influenced by the works of Charles Darwin and Emile Zola, naturalism posited that environment and heredity significantly shaped individuals‘ lives and actions. Naturalist playwrights aimed to observe and represent life with a level of detail akin to scientific study, often depicting characters as products of their surroundings and genetic factors. This approach required meticulous attention to setting, props, and costumes to create an immersive and believable world on stage.

Naturalism often presented a more deterministic view of humanity, suggesting that individuals have limited control over their destinies due to the overpowering influence of environmental and hereditary factors. This perspective allowed for a deeper exploration of the character's motivations, giving audiences insight into why people behave the way they do. Plays like Emile Zola's "Thérèse Raquin" or Maxim Gorky's "The Lower Depths" exemplify naturalism's focus on the darker aspects of human existence, such as poverty, vice, and moral decay, thus encouraging viewers to engage in critical reflection about the conditions and structures of society.

The shift towards realism and naturalism revolutionised the expectations of both playwrights and audiences. As the demand for authentic representation grew, there was a corresponding increase in the complexity and depth of character development. Characters were no longer mere archetypes or symbols; they became multidimensional beings whose psychological depth needed careful crafting. This led to more intricate plotlines and nuanced storytelling as playwrights endeavoured to depict the full spectrum of human emotions and interactions.

Audiences, in turn, began to expect more sophisticated and thought-provoking content from theatrical productions. Rather than seeking mere entertainment, theatregoers increasingly looked to plays for insights into the human condition and reflections on societal issues. The engagement with more profound themes prompted more significant discussions and debates outside the theatre, illustrating the influential role of drama in shaping public consciousness and attitudes.

Notable plays from this era captivated audiences and sparked essential conversations about various facets of society. Henrik Ibsen's "Ghosts," for example, tackled controversial subjects such as venereal disease, incest, and euthanasia, which were considered taboo at the time. By confronting these issues head-on, Ibsen provoked a critical examination of social norms and moral standards, pushing the boundaries of acceptable discourse in the public sphere.

Anton Chekhov's "The Seagull" is another quintessential example that highlights the subtleties of human psychology and interpersonal relationships. Through its exploration of unfulfilled desires, creative aspirations, and existential disillusionment, the play delved into the inner workings of its characters' minds. Chekhov's masterful use of subtext allowed for layers of meaning to be conveyed through seemingly mundane dialogue, encouraging audiences to read between the lines and uncover the underlying tensions and conflicts.

These groundbreaking works were crucial in elevating theatre's status from amusement to a respected form of artistic and intellectual expression. By effectively addressing contemporary social issues and providing realistic portrayals of everyday life, realism and naturalism, they bridged the gap between the stage and real life, making theatre an influential platform for change and introspection.

Key Figures: Ibsen, Chekhov, Strindberg

Several essential playwrights have significantly contributed to modern drama with their unique styles and thought-provoking themes. Their works challenged conventional norms and continue to influence contemporary theatre. Prominent among these figures are Henrik Ibsen, Anton Chekhov, and August Strindberg.

Often called the father of modern drama, Henrik Ibsen revolutionised theatre by focusing on personal and societal conflicts. His plays introduced complex female protagonists who grappled with issues seldom addressed on stage. For example, in "A Doll's House," Ibsen explores the struggles of Nora Helmer, a woman trapped in a restrictive marriage and seeking autonomy. This groundbreaking work not only highlighted the constraints faced by women but also questioned the existing social norms. Ibsen's emphasis on individual struggles against societal expectations opened up new avenues for character development and narrative depth in drama.

Focusing on psychological realism, Anton Chekhov brought a different dimension to modern drama. His characters were deeply complex, reflecting the intricacies of human nature. Unlike traditional plays that relied on dramatic actions and plot twists, Chekhov's works emphasised emotional subtleties and unspoken desires. In plays like "The Seagull" and "Uncle Vanya," Chekhov employed subtext in dialogue, allowing the audience to read between the lines and understand the true motivations and feelings of the characters. This technique brought a sense of authenticity to his work, capturing the essence of real-life interactions.

Chekhov's portrayal of mundane experiences and internal conflicts resonated strongly with audiences, making his plays enduringly relevant. Subtext has become a staple in modern playwriting, offering actors and directors rich material to explore. Through his observational style, Chekhov provided a mirror to the audience, encouraging them to reflect on their own lives and relationships.

Another influential figure, August Strindberg, blended psychological insight with symbolic elements in his plays. His exploration of internal conflicts and existential themes set his work apart. In "Miss Julie," Strindberg delves into the power dynamics and class struggles between an aristocratic woman and her servant, highlighting psychological and societal tensions. The symbolic undertones in his works allowed for multiple layers of interpretation, inviting audiences to ponder more profound philosophical questions about human existence and identity.

Strindberg's innovative use of symbolism paved the way for future playwrights to experiment with abstract concepts and representations on stage. His ability to intertwine the psychological with the symbolic created a rich tapestry of meaning, enhancing the impact and depth of his narratives. The existential themes he explored remain profoundly relevant, prompting audiences to consider their place in the world and the nature of their consciousness.

The techniques and themes Ibsen, Chekhov, and Strindberg pioneered have impacted contemporary drama. Their contributions extend beyond their works, shaping the practices and approaches of modern playwrights. Challenging established conventions and delving into complex human experiences set the stage for a more nuanced and reflective form of theatre.

Ibsen's introduction of strong, multifaceted female characters inspires playwrights to create roles that reflect women's diverse experiences. The societal critiques embedded in his plays encourage writers to address current issues with similar boldness and honesty. Chekhov's emphasis on psychological realism and subtext has become a foundational element of modern playwriting, guiding dramatists to craft more authentic and relatable characters. The subtlety with which he approached emotional depth offers a model for exploring internal landscapes without overt exposition.

Strindberg's integration of symbolic and existential elements provides a framework for contemporary playwrights to incorporate abstract ideas and profound themes into their works. His explorations of identity and consciousness resonate in today's theatre, where existential questions and psychological complexity are frequently central themes. Modern dramatists draw on Strindberg's legacy to weave intricate narratives that challenge audiences intellectually and emotionally.

Expressionist Movements

Expressionism emerged as a revolutionary movement in drama, reshaping the boundaries of theatrical conventions by emphasising emotional experience over realistic representation. This approach allowed playwrights to delve into the depths of human emotion and present an alternative perspective on truth. By utilising exaggeration and distortion, expressionist works aim to convey the inner realities of characters, often presenting truth through a more subjective lens.

One of expressionism's significant aspects is its use of exaggerated and distorted elements to showcase emotional reality. Instead of focusing on the external world as it is, expressionist plays often depict exaggerated settings, characters, and actions that reflect individuals' psychological states. This method allows audiences to see beyond the surface and understand the emotional underpinnings that drive human behaviour. For example, oversized props or exaggerated gestures can symbolise the overwhelming nature of certain emotions or societal pressures.

A prime example of expressionism in drama is Elmer Rice's play "The Adding Machine." Rice employs bold imagery and symbolic elements in this work to critique society's increasing mechanisation and dehumanisation. The protagonist, Mr. Zero, represents the average person trapped in a monotonous, machine-like existence. The play's surreal and distorted setting emphasises the disconnect between the individual's humanity and the impersonal forces of modern society. Rice highlights the emotional and psychological impact of living in a mechanised world through this exaggerated portrayal, urging audiences to reflect on their lives and societal structures.

Expressionist works are known for highlighting characters' inner turmoil, making them relatable on an emotional level. Rather than depicting characters as rational beings driven by clear motivations, expressionist plays often focus on the chaotic and conflicting emotions within the human psyche. This approach makes characters appear more complex and multifaceted, reflecting people's genuine struggles in real life. By presenting characters grappling with intense emotions, expressionist drama creates a profound connection with the audience, who can see their fears, desires, and uncertainties mirrored on stage.

Expressionism also challenges audiences to confront their feelings and experiences. By presenting a heightened reality, these plays push viewers out of their comfort zones and encourage them to engage with the material on a deeper emotional level. The exaggerated portrayals force audiences to question the nature of truth and reality, prompting introspection about their lives and societal norms. This engagement with the audience's emotions makes expressionist drama a powerful social and personal reflection tool.

Moreover, the movement provides an alternative perspective on what constitutes truth in drama. Traditional forms of drama often emphasise a linear narrative and objective reality, but expressionism breaks away from these conventions. Expressionist plays offer a more nuanced understanding of truth by presenting multiple layers of reality and focusing on the subjective experience. This alternative approach allows for a richer exploration of human emotions and experiences, showcasing the complexity of the human condition.

Expressionist techniques have had a lasting influence on modern theatre, expanding the possibilities for how stories can be told on stage. The movement paved the way for other avant-garde and experimental forms of drama, encouraging playwrights and directors to explore new storytelling methods. The emphasis on emotional experience and subjective reality continues to inform contemporary theatre, inspiring artists to push the boundaries of traditional narrative structures and present innovative, thought-provoking works.

Elmer Rice's "The Adding Machine" is a testament to the enduring power of expressionism in drama. By critiquing modern society through bold imagery and distorted reality, Rice captures the emotional essence of his characters and delivers a poignant commentary on the human experience. This blend of emotional depth and social critique is a hallmark of expressionist drama, demonstrating the movement's capacity to resonate with audiences across different eras.

Absurdist Movements

Absurdism emerged as a radical response to the perceived inherent meaninglessness of life, gaining prominence in the mid-20th century. This movement sought to expand the boundaries of drama by delving into existential questions that traditional forms often avoided. The play "Waiting for Godot" by Samuel Beckett is frequently cited as a quintessential example of absurdist theatre. In this work, two characters, Vladimir and Estragon, wait endlessly for someone named Godot, who ultimately never arrives. This scenario encapsulates the essence of absurdism: the futile search for meaning in an incomprehensible world.

Absurdist plays often depict characters grappling against incomprehensible circumstances, mirroring many people's existential dilemmas in modern life. These works present situations where logic breaks down, leaving characters to navigate a chaotic and unpredictable environment. For instance, in "The Bald Soprano" by Eugène Ionesco, conversations between characters become increasingly nonsensical, reflecting the breakdown of communication and meaning. Absurdism underscores human existence's disjointed and often irrational nature through these narratives.

One of the most compelling aspects of absurdism is its challenge to audiences to confront profound questions about purpose and human connection. Rather than providing clear answers or resolutions, absurdist plays compel viewers to engage introspectively. They invite the audience to question their existence and the societal structures they inhabit. The lack of conventional plots or character development does not signify a lack of depth but instead directs attention to the philosophical underpinnings of the narrative. For example, Beckett's minimalistic setting and sparse dialogue in "Waiting for Godot" force the audience to focus on existential themes rather than being distracted by elaborate scenery or action.

Themes of alienation and disillusionment are central to absurdist drama and remain highly relevant in contemporary society. Absurdist playwrights depict characters who experience profound feelings of isolation and disconnect from the world around them. In Harold Pinter's "The Dumb Waiter," two assassins wait in a claustrophobic basement for their next assignment, communicating through fragmented sentences and cryptic messages. This scenario highlights the pervasive alienation and estrangement that can arise in modern life. Such themes resonate with individuals' experiences of social disconnection and the search for meaning within a seemingly indifferent universe.

Moreover, absurdist works provoke a continuous reevaluation of societal norms by scrutinising the conventions that govern everyday life. By presenting scenarios that defy logical explanations, absurdist playwrights question the validity and relevance of established norms and values. The disruption of conventional narratives allows for critically examining what is typically accepted without question. In Ionesco's "Rhinoceros," the inhabitants of a small town gradually transform into rhinoceroses, symbolising the spread of conformity and loss of individuality. The play challenges audiences to reflect on their susceptibility to societal pressures and the consequences of uncritical acceptance of dominant ideologies.

In addition to challenging existing norms, absurdism offers a unique lens through which to view the complexities of human relationships. Absurdist plays often explore the tenuous and ambiguous nature of connections between individuals. The interactions between characters frequently reveal the limitations and failures of language as a tool for genuine communication. In Edward Albee's "The Zoo Story," the seemingly mundane encounter between two men in Central Park escalates into a violent confrontation, exposing the underlying tensions and misunderstandings characterising human relationships. Through such narratives, absurdism emphasises the difficulty and often futility of achieving proper understanding and connection with others.

The enduring relevance of absurdism lies in its ability to address timeless existential concerns while adapting to modern society's evolving context. As contemporary audiences grapple with questions of identity, purpose, and connection in an increasingly complex world, the themes explored in absurdist drama maintain their significance. The movement's emphasis on the absurdity of human existence provides a powerful framework for examining life's disorienting and often contradictory nature.

Furthermore, absurdist theatre has inspired subsequent generations of playwrights and artists to experiment with form and content, pushing the boundaries of what is considered possible within the realm of drama. The legacy of absurdism can be seen in various contemporary works that challenge traditional narrative structures and explore unconventional themes. Playwrights such as Tom Stoppard and Sarah Kane have drawn on absurdist principles to create innovative and thought-provoking pieces that continue to engage and challenge audiences.

Contemporary Trends in Modern Drama

One of the pivotal aspects of modern drama is the increasing emphasis on diverse voices and perspectives. This shift enriches contemporary playwriting by reflecting a broad spectrum of cultural and societal viewpoints. As society becomes more globalised, the theatre has responded by incorporating stories from different cultures, ethnicities, genders, and social backgrounds. This diversity allows audiences to see themselves represented on stage, fostering empathy and understanding between various communities.

For example, playwrights like Lynn Nottage and Quiara Alegría Hudes have gained acclaim for their compelling portrayals of African-American and Latino experiences, respectively. Nottage's works, such as "Sweat" and "Ruined," delve into the lives of marginalised groups, shedding light on social issues like economic disparity and conflict in war-torn regions. Similarly, Hudes‘ "Water by the Spoonful" explores themes of addiction, identity, and reconciliation within a Puerto Rican family. By presenting these unique perspectives, contemporary drama encourages audiences to confront and contemplate issues they may not encounter daily.

Another notable trend in modern drama is the integration of multimedia elements, which opens new avenues for storytelling and audience engagement. Projections, video, soundscapes, and interactive technology can create immersive theatrical experiences that traditional methods might not achieve. These elements enhance productions' visual and auditory appeal and allow for innovative narrative techniques.

Take, for instance, the work of British playwright and director Robert Lepage, known for his avant-garde approach to theatre. His production "The Blue Dragon" employs elaborate projections and moving sets to transport audiences across various landscapes, both real and imagined. Similarly, the musical "Dear Evan Hansen" uses social media graphics and live texting displays to reflect the protagonist's digital life, making the story particularly resonant with younger audiences familiar with online communication. This fusion of traditional drama with modern technology can captivate viewers, making theatrical events more relevant to today's tech-savvy society.

Contemporary plays often tackle pressing social issues such as climate change, identity, and mental health, provoking thought and inspiring action. Playwrights increasingly use their platforms to address urgent topics that resonate deeply with audiences, encouraging discussions beyond the theatre.

For instance, Duncan Macmillan's "Lungs" deals explicitly with climate anxiety, as a couple debates whether to bring a child into a world threatened by environmental disaster. The play's raw dialogue and intimate setting compel audiences to grapple with their environmental concerns and responsibilities. Another example is the musical "Next to Normal," which examines mental illness and its impact on a suburban family. Its candid exploration of bipolar disorder and grief challenges societal stigmas around mental health, fostering greater awareness and empathy.

Modern adaptations of classical texts ensure timeless themes remain accessible and relatable to today's audience. By reinterpreting classic works through a contemporary lens, playwrights and directors can make age-old stories relevant to current issues and sensibilities.

Consider Simon Stone's adaptation of Euripides' "Medea." Stone sets the Greek tragedy in a modern-day context, transforming Medea into a contemporary woman dealing with divorce and custody battles. This choice makes the ancient text more accessible and emotionally engaging for contemporary audiences. Similarly, Branden Jacobs-Jenkins' "An Octoroon" reimagines Dion Boucicault's 19th-century melodrama "The Octoroon" by blending historical and modern elements to critique race relations, both past and present. These adaptations bridge the gap between the old and the new, demonstrating how timeless human experiences can transcend temporal boundaries.

What We Learnt

This chapter has explored the transition from classical drama to modern realism and naturalism, highlighting how these movements reshaped theatre by focusing on authentic depictions of everyday life and societal issues. We examined the contributions of key playwrights like Henrik Ibsen and Anton Chekhov, who used their works to address pressing social themes such as class struggles, gender roles, and family dynamics. Naturalism's deeper dive into human behaviour through scientific lenses further advanced this trend, emphasising environmental and hereditary influences on characters' lives.

As we conclude, realism and naturalism brought about a new era of complexity and depth in theatrical storytelling. Characters became more multidimensional, plotlines grew richer, and audiences sought plays beyond entertainment to provoke thought and social reflection. This shift not only elevated the status of theatre but also solidified its role as a medium for exploring and challenging contemporary issues. Through their realistic portrayals and critical insights, these dramatic forms have left an enduring legacy that continues to influence modern drama.

CHAPTER V

Elements of Drama: Plot and Structure

The elements of drama, particularly plot and structure, are crucial in shaping the narrative and engaging the audience. These components serve as the blueprint for any play, directing the storyline flow while guiding character development and thematic exploration. By deconstructing the framework of dramatic works, we can better understand how these elements work together to create compelling and memorable narratives.

This chapter will explore how the exposition sets the stage by introducing key characters, settings, and initial conflicts essential for providing context. We then delve into the inciting incident, which propels the protagonist into the main action and ignites the plot's progression. Following this, the climax is examined as the turning point of heightened tension and pivotal decisions, leading to the falling action that begins resolving these tensions. Finally, we analyse the resolution and outcome, revealing the consequences of the characters' journeys and solidifying the thematic messages of the drama. Through this comprehensive examination, readers will better appreciate the intricate mechanics behind compelling storytelling in dramatic works.

Exposition and Inciting Incident

Establishing the setting and conflict early in a dramatic work is crucial for guiding the audience through the narrative. Exposition is the initial phase of a drama, where essential information about characters, setting, and background is introduced. Understanding this component is necessary for providing context and laying the groundwork for the plot.

In the exposition, the playwright introduces pivotal characters, their relationships, and the setting—an important aspect that helps situate the story within a specific time and place. For instance, in Arthur Miller's "The Crucible," the opening scene in Reverend Parris's house immediately informs the audience of Salem, Massachusetts's historical and puritanical setting, during the witch trials. This sets the tone and provides a backdrop against which the ensuing drama unfolds.

Moreover, the exposition includes background information that gives insight into the characters' motivations and circumstances. This understanding is vital for grasping the initial conflicts that drive the plot. In William Shakespeare's "Romeo and Juliet," the prologue sets up the long-standing feud between the Montagues and Capulets, establishing an immediate source of tension that propels the action forward. Without this initial setup, the audience might struggle to comprehend the reasons behind the characters' actions and the significance of their decisions.

The exposition is the foundation upon which the rest of the plot develops, ensuring the audience grasps the initial conflicts. These conflicts are often introduced subtly through dialogue and minor incidents rather than overt action. For example, in Henrik Ibsen's "A Doll's House," the seemingly mundane conversations between Nora and her husband Torvald reveal underlying tensions in their marriage and hint at their financial troubles. Such revelations prepare the audience for the more significant conflicts later in the narrative.

Furthermore, the exposition is instrumental in building connections between the audience and the characters. By illustrating the circumstances and motives of the characters, the playwright encourages the audience to empathise with them. In Tennessee Williams's "The Glass Menagerie," the opening monologue by Tom Wingfield invites the audience to view the subsequent events from his perspective, fostering a sense of intimacy and understanding. Through shared experiences and emotions, the audience becomes invested in the characters' journeys.

As the plot progresses, the carefully crafted exposition prepares the audience for the unfolding thematic elements. For example, the introduction of Willy Loman in Arthur Miller's "Death of a Salesman" sets the stage for exploring success, failure, and disillusionment themes. The early glimpses into Willy's life highlight his dreams and struggles, foreshadowing the central issues that the play will address. By offering these initial insights, the exposition signals to the audience what to expect thematically, enhancing their engagement with the story.

In addition to providing context and preparing the audience for the plot, the exposition often hints at the broader thematic concerns that will be explored throughout the drama. This subtle foreshadowing allows the audience to anticipate and recognise recurring motifs and deeper meanings as the narrative unfolds. For instance, the opening scenes of Lorraine Hansberry's "A Raisin in the Sun" introduce the Younger family's aspiration for a better life and their societal challenges, themes that resonate throughout the play.

They effectively introduce the setting and primary conflicts early on, which offers several advantages. It allows the audience to become oriented within the world of the play, making it easier to follow the storyline. When the audience understands the fundamental conflicts and setting from the beginning, they can focus on the development of the plot and characters without being distracted by confusion over fundamental details. Additionally, this early establishment of the dramatic framework can enhance the story's emotional impact as viewers become more deeply invested in the characters' fates and the resolutions of their conflicts.

An adequate exposition balances providing necessary information and maintaining the audience's interest. Overloading the audience with details can be counterproductive and lead to disengagement. Instead, playwrights skillfully weave background information into the narrative flow, allowing the story to unfold organically. An exemplary model of this technique is found in Anton Chekhov's "The Cherry Orchard," where the exposition subtly reveals the financial troubles of the Ranevsky family while simultaneously immersing the audience in the poetic ambience of the cherry orchard itself.

Defining Inciting Incident

The inciting incident is a crucial component of any dramatic work, serving as the moment that propels the protagonist into action or conflict. Without this pivotal event, the narrative would lack direction and urgency, leaving characters stagnant and the audience disengaged. By analysing the role and impact of the inciting incident, we can better understand how it serves as the backbone of the plot and structure in drama.

The inciting incident acts as a catalyst for the main narrative, pushing characters into motion and dilemmas. It often introduces a problem or challenge that disrupts the protagonist's ordinary life, forcing them to make decisions and take actions that drive the story forward. For example, in William Shakespeare's "Hamlet," the inciting incident occurs when the ghost of Hamlet's father reveals that Claudius murdered him. This revelation compels Hamlet to seek revenge, setting the entire plot into motion. Without the ghost's appearance, Hamlet would have no reason to confront his uncle, and the subsequent events of the play would never unfold.

Moreover, the inciting incident marks the transition from ordinary life to a disruptive event, heightening anticipation for the audience. This shift creates a sense of excitement and intrigue, as viewers are eager to see how characters will react and what consequences will arise from the disruption. In Arthur Miller's "The Crucible," the inciting incident happens when the girls are caught dancing in the woods, and accusations of witchcraft begin to surface. This event shatters the normalcy of the Puritan community and plunges its members into chaos and paranoia. The audience becomes invested in the storyline, anticipating how the fervour will escalate and impact the characters involved.

In addition to propelling the narrative and heightening anticipation, the inciting incident opens up thematic discussions that will be explored throughout the play. By introducing key themes early on, the playwright sets the stage for deeper exploration and reflection as the story progresses. For instance, in Lorraine Hansberry's "A Raisin in the Sun," the inciting incident occurs when the Younger family learns they will receive a $10,000 insurance check following the death of Walter Sr. This financial windfall sparks dreams and conflicts among family members, raising themes of racial identity, economic struggle, and generational aspirations. As the play unfolds, these themes are further examined through the characters‘ actions and choices.

Climax and Falling Action

The climax stands as the most crucial juncture in any dramatic narrative. It serves as the turning point where tension reaches its zenith, acting as a central piece around which the rest of the story evolves. Understanding how to identify the climax is essential for fully appreciating a drama’s structure and emotional impact. Generally marked by heightened emotions and pivotal decisions, the climax often occurs toward the latter part of the play, propelling the narrative towards its ultimate resolution.

One effective method to identify the climax is to analyse the buildup of tension throughout the plot. The events leading to this peak will typically intensify, creating suspense and anticipation. For instance, in William Shakespeare’s Romeo and Juliet, the climax occurs when Romeo kills Tybalt. This act of violence heightens the stakes, shifting the narrative from romantic tragedy to impending doom. One can pinpoint the climax more accurately by recognising the escalating conflict sequence.

Moreover, the climax represents critical choices and developments that significantly alter the story’s direction. These choices often have far-reaching consequences, profoundly affecting the protagonist and other characters.

In Arthur Miller's "The Crucible," the climax is reached when John Proctor decides to confess to witchcraft, only to retract it, choosing integrity over life. This turning point not only shapes the character's fate but also serves as a commentary on the themes of honour and moral courage.

Engaging the audience deeply, the climax offers a moment of catharsis and excitement. It's a juncture where the audience's emotional investment pays off, relieving the building tension. A well-crafted climax will evoke a range of emotions—fear, joy, sorrow, or anger—drawing the audience into the heart of the drama. For example, in Lorraine Hansberry's "A Raisin in the Sun," the climax occurs when Walter Lee rejects Mr. Lindner's offer, reclaiming his family's pride and dignity. This decision elicits strong emotional responses, emphasising the themes of identity and resilience.

Additionally, the climax mirrors the protagonist's journey, shedding light on their growth or decline through pivotal actions. It is a revealing lens, offering insights into the character's development and internal struggles. Take the case of Willy Loman in Arthur Miller's "Death of a Salesman." The climax is reached when Willy decides to end his own life, believing that his death will provide financial security for his family. This tragic decision highlights Willy's disillusionment and desperation, encapsulating his character arc.

In summary, understanding the climax involves more than just identifying the most exciting part of a drama. It requires a deep analysis of the narrative's structure, the critical choices made by characters, and the emotional engagement elicited from the audience. Through these elements, the climax is a pivotal moment that defines the overall arc of the story, revealing character transformations and thematic impacts that resonate long after the final curtain falls.

Understanding Falling Action

Post-climax events often called the falling action, are essential in concluding a dramatic work. Once the climax—the peak of emotional intensity—is reached, the narrative begins its descent, addressing unresolved tensions and setting the stage for resolution. Understanding this phase is crucial for both creators and audience members as it provides clarity and closure following the heightened excitement of the climax.

One of the primary functions of post-climax events is to start tying up loose ends. These plot segments begin to address and resolve conflicts throughout the story. Characters embroiled in tension and turmoil during the climax now navigate the aftermath. Their responses to climactic events are crucial; they reflect growth, relationship shifts, and deeper insights into their personalities. For instance, if a character faces a moral dilemma during the climax, their actions in the falling action reveal how they internalise and respond to the consequences of their choices.

This progression helps maintain audience engagement subtly but effectively. The transition from high tension to eventual closure allows the audience to process the unfolding events while still being invested in the characters' journeys. It's a delicate balance—too abrupt a shift can feel jarring, disrupting the immersive experience. Conversely, a too-drawn-out falling action may result in a loss of interest. Drama relies heavily on pacing, and post-climax events are vital to sustaining momentum until the end.

Moreover, post-climax events serve as an opportunity to reinforce themes and character arcs. Themes that might have been hinted at or developed during the earlier parts of the narrative gain more depth through the characters‘ reflections and decisions post-climax. This reinforces the story's natural progression and enhances the audience's emotional satisfaction. For example, a theme of redemption can become more poignant as characters seek forgiveness or make amends for past actions during the falling action.

Character arcs, which track individuals' personal growth and changes within the story, reach their maturation during this phase. If a character begins the story with significant flaws or internal conflicts, the falling action allows these traits to be addressed and evolved. A protagonist who struggles with self-doubt might demonstrate newfound confidence when confronting the consequences of the climax, thus completing their arc in a manner that feels authentic and satisfying.

In addition, post-climax events offer a platform for thematic exploration without the intense pressure of the climax. With the central conflict resolved, there's room for subtler, reflective moments where characters and themes can resonate more deeply with the audience. Visualising these scenes as the calm after a storm can be helpful; the narrative winds down, allowing for reflection and contemplation that enriches the overall impact of the drama.

To illustrate these concepts, consider William Shakespeare's "Romeo and Juliet." After the protagonists‘ double suicides, the remaining characters face the consequences of the family feud that led to such tragic outcomes. The falling action shows the families' reactions, grief, and reconciliation. The thematic elements of love, conflict, and fate are underscored as the plot moves toward resolution, culminating in a sense of closure that feels earned and impactful.

Similarly, in Arthur Miller's "The Crucible," the post-climax events follow John Proctor's refusal to confess to witchcraft falsely. His decision leads to his execution, but the subsequent actions of the other characters and the town's response provide insight into themes of integrity, hysteria, and redemption. The falling action here serves not only to wrap up the narrative but also to drive home the core messages of the play.

Understanding the role of post-climax events in drama is pivotal for anyone studying or creating dramatic works. Whether one aims to write compelling plays, analyse existing ones, or perform them, recognising how these events foster resolution, maintain engagement, and reinforce themes enhances the appreciation and effectiveness of the narrative. By carefully crafting this phase, playwrights ensure their stories deliver a satisfying and thought-provoking experience, leaving a lasting impression on their audience.

Resolution and Denouement

It's essential to delve into the various aspects of resolution to analyse how a drama's outcomes offer closure and insight into character arcs and thematic meanings. A dramatic work's resolution ends the central conflict, providing clarity and closure to the narrative. It is where the story's loose ends are tied up, the fate of the characters is revealed, and the themes explored throughout the play are reinforced or subverted.

Exploring Resolution: The conclusion of the central conflict is crucial as it provides a sense of fulfilment and completeness to the narrative. The resolution helps the audience understand the story's outcome and the characters' journey in many plays. For instance, in William Shakespeare's "Romeo and Juliet," the resolution occurs when the feuding families reconcile after the tragic deaths of the young lovers. This resolution not only concludes the central conflict but also reinforces the theme of the destructive nature of familial hatred.

Providing finality to character journeys is another critical function of the resolution. By the end of the play, audiences expect to see where the characters' paths have led them. This ensures that viewers understand the motivations and outcomes of the characters' actions. For example, in Arthur Miller's "The Crucible," John Proctor's ultimate decision to maintain his integrity, even at the cost of his life, provides a powerful conclusion to his character arc. The resolution highlights Proctor's transformation and solidifies his role as a tragic hero who chooses truth over falsehood.

Revealing the consequences of characters' choices offers audiences thought-provoking reflections on morality and ethics. Dramatic works often mirror society, allowing viewers to ponder the ramifications of actions taken by the characters. In Henrik Ibsen's "A Doll's House," Nora Helmer's decision to leave her husband and children at the end of the play underscores the consequences of seeking individual freedom in a restrictive society. The resolution prompts audiences to reflect on the ethical dimensions of Nora's choice and the societal norms that necessitated such drastic action.

Resolutions also play a significant role in reinforcing or subverting initial themes, prompting audience reactions and interpretations. A well-crafted resolution can either affirm the themes introduced earlier in the play or challenge them, leading viewers to reconsider their initial assumptions. In Tennessee Williams' "A Streetcar Named Desire," the resolution subverts the theme of illusion versus reality. While Blanche DuBois seeks refuge in her illusions, the harsh reality of her situation ultimately prevails. The resolution forces the audience to confront the brutal truths about Blanche's life and the society she inhabits.

Defining Subplots: While the primary focus of a resolution is the main storyline, it is also essential to address any subplots. Subplots add depth and complexity to the narrative, and their resolutions contribute to the overall sense of closure. For example, in Shakespeare's "King Lear," the subplot involving Gloucester and his sons, Edgar and Edmund, parallels the main plot and enhances the themes of betrayal and redemption. The resolution of this subplot, with Edgar defeating Edmund and Gloucester's eventual reconciliation with Edgar, provides additional layers of meaning to the central narrative.

Understanding Denouement: The denouement, or the final part of a dramatic work, is integral to the resolution. It is the moment when the tension dissipates, and the aftermath of the central conflict is explored. In Anton Chekhov's "The Cherry Orchard," the denouement focuses on selling the family estate and the characters' departure. This moment of reflection allows the audience to absorb the story's emotional impact and contemplate the more prominent themes of change and loss.

In summary, the resolution is a vital element of drama that offers closure and insight into character arcs and thematic meanings. By concluding the central conflict, providing finality to character journeys, revealing the consequences of choices, and reinforcing or subverting themes, the resolution ensures that audiences leave the theatre with a deeper understanding of the narrative. Additionally, addressing subplots and incorporating a poignant denouement further enriches the audience's experience, resolving a vital component of the dramatic structure.

What We Learnt

This chapter delved into the fundamental components of dramatic works, emphasising the significance of plot and structure in guiding the audience through a narrative journey. By illustrating how exposition sets the stage with essential background information, we explored how introducing key elements like characters, setting, and initial conflicts is the foundation for any drama. The role of the inciting incident was examined as a catalyst that propels the protagonist into action, creating urgency and driving the plot forward. Furthermore, the significance of the climax and falling action was highlighted, demonstrating how these pivotal moments escalate tension and lead to the resolution, concluding the characters' journeys and thematic explorations.

Understanding these frameworks allows readers and creators to appreciate the intricacies of dramatic storytelling. Recognising the interplay between exposition, rising action, climax, and resolution enhances one's ability to analyse and craft compelling narratives. For students aiming to deepen their literary analysis, educators seeking to enrich their teaching methods, or theatre enthusiasts desiring a greater connection with dramatic works, grasping these structural elements is invaluable. Through this chapter, we have equipped our audience with the tools to engage with plays critically, fostering a deeper appreciation for the art of drama and its impact on audiences.

CHAPTER VI

Character Development in Drama

Character development in drama is a crucial aspect of storytelling that captivates audiences and drives narratives. The creation and growth of characters are essential in exploring themes, revealing motivations, and engaging readers or viewers with the unfolding plot. Understanding how characters evolve and influence a story can significantly enhance the appreciation of dramatic works.

This chapter delves into the various types of characters commonly found in drama, including protagonists, antagonists, and foils. It explores methods of characterisation that playwrights use to bring these roles to life, such as direct and indirect characterisation. Additionally, the chapter examines character arcs and transformations, highlighting how characters change throughout a narrative. By understanding these elements, readers will better appreciate the complexity and depth of character interactions in drama, leading to richer analysis and more meaningful engagement with the material.

Types of Characters: Protagonists, Antagonists, Foils

The subpoint for this chapter aims to help readers identify and differentiate between crucial character types, enhancing their understanding of the roles characters play in driving the narrative and thematic depth.

Firstly, protagonists are central characters around whom the story revolves. In drama, protagonists not only drive the plot but also embody the core themes of the play. A protagonist's growth is typically significant, showcasing a transformation that reflects the underlying messages of the narrative. For example, Hamlet in Shakespeare's "Hamlet" evolves from a brooding prince burdened by grief to a figure ready to confront his fate. This evolution highlights themes such as revenge, mortality, and madness.

Antagonists serve as the opposing forces to the protagonists. These characters are crucial because they catalyse the protagonist's development, pushing them into situations that demand change and growth. Without the antagonist, little conflict would propel the story forward. Consider Iago in Shakespeare's "Othello"; his actions directly challenge Othello, leading to tragic outcomes. Iago provides insight into themes like jealousy, manipulation, and trust, revealing more profound layers of conflict within the narrative.

Foils, on the other hand, are characters designed to contrast with the protagonists. They highlight specific traits and illuminate broader themes such as identity, morality, and growth. For instance, in Mary Shelley's "Frankenstein," Henry Clerval is a foil to Victor Frankenstein. Where Victor is obsessed with ambition and creation, Henry represents empathy and human connection. This contrast helps readers understand the consequences of unchecked ambition and the importance of human relationships.

Understanding these character roles enhances the engagement with dramatic works. A guideline for identifying these character types in familiar works can greatly benefit readers. Let's consider Arthur Miller's "The Crucible."

To identify the protagonist, look for the character who undergoes significant internal change. In "The Crucible," John Proctor serves as the protagonist. He evolves from a flawed individual to someone who redeems himself through confession and sacrifice. To recognise antagonists, seek out those who create obstacles. Abigail Williams exemplifies this role by instigating the witch trials and manipulating others, thus driving the central conflict. Lastly, foils can be discerned through their contrasting qualities. Reverend Hale, initially a firm believer in witchcraft, acts as a foil to much of the hysteria, as he eventually opposes the trials and symbolises reason against mass paranoia.

Readers can better appreciate character dynamics and thematic exploration by identifying these character types across various dramas. This process involves attention to the characters' roles and actions throughout the narrative. For example, in Tennessee Williams' "A Streetcar Named Desire," Blanche DuBois stands out as the protagonist, her complex character unravelling as the plot progresses. Stanley Kowalski emerges as the antagonist, creating tension and conflict that drives Blanche towards her downfall. At the same time, Stella serves as a foil, her grounded nature contrasting sharply with Blanche's fragile mental state, highlighting themes of reality versus illusion.

Recognising the different character types not only aids in understanding the narrative structure but also enriches critical analysis. When watching or reading a play, focus on how each character type influences the story's progression. This approach can lead to a more thoughtful interpretation of the material. Take Henrik Ibsen's "A Doll's House." Nora Helmer embodies the protagonist role, her journey reflecting the struggles of self-identity within the confines of societal expectations. While seemingly supportive, Torvald Helmer acts as an antagonist, his patronising behaviour perpetuating Nora's internal conflict. Meanwhile, Kristine Linde functions as a foil, her pragmatic approach to life highlighting Nora's eventual awakening and desire for independence.

By examining well-known dramas through the lens of these character types, one gains valuable insights into storytelling mechanisms. For young adults studying literature, this method enables a more precise grasp of how characters contribute to the work's themes and emotional impact. This framework offers educators a structured way to teach character analysis, providing students with concrete tools to dissect and discuss literary works. Understanding these roles can enhance performance quality for theatre enthusiasts, allowing actors to delve deeper into their characters' motivations and relationships.

Methods of Characterisation

Playwrights use various methods to develop characters in drama, enriching the audience's understanding of the narrative and deepening their engagement with the story. Characterisation is a vital aspect of drama, as it shapes how the audience perceives and relates to the characters on stage.

One primary method of characterisation is direct characterisation. The playwright explicitly describes the characters' traits and motivations in this approach. This technique allows for the quick establishment of essential character details, enabling the audience to grasp key aspects of the characters without ambiguity. For instance, a playwright might introduce a character as "a wealthy and proud man" or "a humble and kind-hearted woman." This straightforward description gives the audience immediate insight into the character's nature and sets expectations for their behaviour and role in the narrative. Direct characterisation is instrumental in plays with limited time for expansive character development, as it efficiently conveys necessary information.

Indirect characterisation, on the other hand, reveals character traits through actions, thoughts, dialogue, and interactions with different characters. This method engages the audience's critical thinking and interpretation skills, as they must deduce the characters' qualities from their behaviour and choices. For example, instead of stating that a character is brave, a playwright might courageously depict the character facing a dangerous situation. Similarly, a character's internal monologue can reveal their fears, desires, and moral compass. This nuanced approach allows for more complex and layered character portrayals as audiences uncover different facets of the characters over time. Indirect characterisation encourages deeper investment in the narrative as viewers piece together clues to form a comprehensive understanding of each character.

Character speech patterns are another crucial element of characterisation. How characters speak - their choice of words, tone, and mannerisms - can provide significant insights into their background, social status, and internal conflicts. For instance, a character who uses formal, sophisticated language might be perceived as educated or aristocratic. At the same time, one who speaks in colloquial slang might be seen as more down-to-earth or rebellious. Accents and dialects can also reveal a character's regional origin or cultural identity.

Furthermore, speech pattern inconsistencies can indicate a character's internal struggles or hidden aspects. A usually confident character who suddenly stammers may be experiencing doubt or fear. By analysing speech patterns, the audience gains a richer understanding of the characters' identities and the dynamics between them.

Contrasting and paralleling characters is another effective technique to enhance the audience's comprehension of individual traits and broader thematic concerns. Contrasts highlight differences between characters, often emphasising their unique qualities and roles within the narrative. For instance, a protagonist's virtues may be accentuated by placing them alongside an antagonist's vices. This juxtaposition clarifies the protagonist's admirable qualities and intensifies the conflict driving the plot. Conversely, paralleling characters share similar traits or experiences, which can underscore common themes or foster empathy. Two characters from different backgrounds encountering similar challenges might illustrate universal human struggles, reinforcing the play's overarching messages. Through contrasts and parallels, playwrights enrich the storytelling, offering multiple perspectives and deepening the audience's emotional and intellectual engagement.

To analyse direct characterisation effectively, readers should focus on explicit descriptions provided by the playwright. These descriptions are often found in character introductions, stage directions, or dialogue where one character describes another. Readers can look for adjectives and phrases that define physical appearance, personality, and motivations. For example, in Arthur Miller's "The Crucible," Reverend Parris is introduced with clear descriptions that establish his anxious and paranoid nature: "He cut a villainous path... trying to climb up into his ancestor's power."

In the case of indirect characterisation, readers need to pay attention to the characters' actions, thoughts, dialogue, and interactions. They should consider what these elements reveal about the characters' underlying traits and motivations. Observing how characters react to various situations—whether they act bravely, cowardly, honestly, or deceitfully—provides insight into their core attributes. Their private thoughts revealed through soliloquies or monologues, can expose hidden fears or ambitions. Interactions with other characters also shed light on relationships and social dynamics. For instance, Shakespeare's Hamlet offers rich opportunities for analysing indirect characterisation, as Hamlet's soliloquies reveal his inner turmoil and philosophical reflections.

When it comes to character speech patterns, readers should examine the language used by each character. Analysing vocabulary, syntax, and diction can help identify social and educational backgrounds, emotional states, and power dynamics. Characters' speech can also reflect their evolution throughout the play. For instance, in Tennessee Williams' "A Streetcar Named Desire," Blanche DuBois' affected speech suggests her desperation to cling to her genteel past. At the same time, Stanley Kowalski's blunt, unrefined language emphasises his working-class roots and raw masculinity. Changes in speech patterns can indicate character development or psychological shifts, providing deeper layers of meaning to the dialogue.

Readers can create charts or lists to compare characteristics, behaviours, and outcomes for contrasting and paralleling characters. Identifying pairs of characters with opposing or mirroring traits helps clarify the play's thematic explorations. Readers might consider how the differences or similarities between characters serve to highlight central conflicts or reinforce key messages. For example, in Lorraine Hansberry's "A Raisin in the Sun," the contrasts between Walter Lee Younger and George Murchison reveal different attitudes towards African American identity and aspirations, enriching the play's exploration of racial and economic issues.

Character Arcs and Transformations

Character arcs are a fundamental aspect of drama that reveals the development and transformation of characters throughout the narrative. A character arc is the journey a character undergoes, from their initial state at the story's beginning to their resolved state by the end. This transformation is not just physical; it encompasses emotional, psychological, and moral growth. Understanding character arcs provides deeper insight into the thematic depth of a play, illustrating how characters evolve in response to the trials they face.

At its core, a character arc demonstrates change. This change can manifest in various forms, such as personal growth, altered beliefs, or new-found strengths, fundamentally altering the character's role and perspective within the narrative. For instance, in Shakespeare's "Hamlet," the titular character begins as a grieving son seeking revenge but ultimately undergoes profound internal struggles that shape his actions and mindset. The significance of these arcs lies in showing audiences how characters respond to challenges, thus revealing broader themes and messages within the play.

There are several types of character arcs, each contributing uniquely to storytelling. Positive arcs depict a character's progression toward betterment. In these arcs, the character often starts with flaws or deficiencies and grows into a more rounded, capable individual. An example of a positive arc can be seen in Elizabeth Bennet from Jane Austen's Pride and Prejudice. She evolves from prejudiced judgments to a greater understanding and love for Mr. Darcy, showcasing significant personal growth.

Conversely, negative arcs show a character's decline. These arcs may reveal how certain traits or decisions lead to downfall and destruction. Tony Montana in "Scarface" illustrates this, where his ruthless ambition ultimately leads to his tragic demise. Negative arcs underscore themes of hubris, corruption, or moral decay, offering audiences a cautionary tale.

Static arcs present characters who remain fundamentally unchanged throughout the narrative. While they might face numerous obstacles, their core values and beliefs stay intact. Sherlock Holmes is a quintessential static character whose brilliant detective skills and logical approach remain constant despite the mysteries he solves. Static arcs highlight the strength or rigidity of a character's principles, affecting the plot dynamics around them.

Conflict is a pivotal force in driving character transformations. Dramatic tension stems from the clashing desires, goals, or values among characters or within a single character. These conflicts create situations that force characters to make significant decisions, leading to either growth or regression. For example, in Arthur Miller's "The Crucible," John Proctor's internal conflict between maintaining his reputation and confessing to save others causes a profound transformation, culminating in his ultimate decision to act with integrity.

Conflicts often involve external pressures like societal norms or interpersonal relationships that challenge characters' perceptions and decisions. These pressures create the necessary friction that propels characters forward in their arcs. For instance, in Lorraine Hansberry's "A Raisin in the Sun," Walter Lee Younger grapples with economic hardship and familial responsibilities, driving his evolution from frustration to becoming a caring family leader.

Assessing character growth involves reflecting on characters' choices and consequences throughout the play. This evaluation can be done by analysing key scenes where critical decisions occur, noting the motivations behind these decisions and their impacts on the character's journey. It also includes tracking the character's emotional and psychological changes through dialogue, actions, and reactions to events in the plot.

One method to measure growth is to compare a character's state at different points in the narrative. In the beginning, what were their goals, fears, and relationships? Midway through the story, how have these elements shifted due to the unfolding drama? What has the character learned, sacrificed, or achieved by the end? This comparison can illuminate the transformative journey the character undertakes.

Another approach is considering feedback from other characters within the narrative. Often, supporting characters provide insights or critiques that reflect the protagonist's growth. For example, in "To Kill a Mockingbird," Scout Finch's development is mirrored and reinforced by her interactions with Atticus and other figures in Maycomb, helping readers gauge her maturation and changed worldview.

Relationship Dynamics and Interactions

One key element in character development within drama is the exploration of relationships among characters. These relationships significantly impact the character's actions, motivations, and growth throughout the narrative. By examining familial, romantic, and antagonistic dynamics, we can better understand how these interactions shape the characters and propel the story forward.

Familial relationships often lay the foundation for character motivations and actions. For instance, consider the strained relationship between Hamlet and his mother, Gertrude, in Shakespeare's "Hamlet." Hamlet's deep resentment towards his mother's hasty remarriage to Claudius fuels his actions and internal conflict throughout the play. Familial ties can also provide support and a sense of duty, as in Arthur Miller's "Death of a Salesman," where their father's expectations and failures influence Biff and Happy. The family unit is a microcosm of society, reflecting broader themes and conflicts that the characters must navigate.

Romantic relationships, conversely, introduce layers of vulnerability and desire that push characters beyond their comfort zones. In "Romeo and Juliet," the intense love between the titular characters drives them to defy their feuding families, leading to personal and societal transformations. Romantic entanglements can also reveal characters' fears and insecurities, making them more relatable to the audience. For example, in Tennessee Williams‘ "A Streetcar Named Desire," Blanche DuBois's interactions with men expose her deep-seated need for validation and fear of loneliness, driving her to madness.

Antagonistic relationships are pivotal in creating tension and driving the plot. These dynamics often force characters to confront their deepest values and beliefs. In George Orwell's "1984," the protagonist Winston's struggle against the oppressive regime represented by Big Brother highlights the conflict between individual freedom and authoritarian control. This antagonistic relationship is crucial in shaping Winston's actions and ultimate fate. Similarly, in "The Crucible" by Arthur Miller, the antagonism between John Proctor and Abigail Williams intensifies the dramatic tension and underscores the broader themes of truth and integrity versus deception and hysteria.

Relationships not only impact character motivations but also catalyse their growth. Often, it is through these interactions that protagonists evolve and confront their fears. In J.K. Rowling's "Harry Potter" series, Harry's relationships with friends like Hermione and Ron and his mentor, Dumbledore, drive his transformation from an uncertain young boy to a confident leader willing to face Voldemort. These relationships support challenge perceptions and encourage self-reflection, facilitating character development.

Conflict within relationships is another powerful tool in drama that forces characters to make critical choices, revealing their core values and beliefs. In Henrik Ibsen's "A Doll's House," Nora's evolving relationship with her husband Torvald leads her to realise the constraints of her marriage and societal expectations. The conflict climaxes when Nora leaves Torvald, symbolising her quest for identity and independence. Such conflicts compel characters to evaluate their priorities and change accordingly, making the narrative more compelling.

Dialogue is significant in revealing relationship dynamics and providing insights into emotional connections between characters. Through dialogue, playwrights can convey subtext or the underlying meaning behind the spoken words, which adds depth to the interactions. For instance, in George Bernard Shaw's Pygmalion, the conversations between Henry Higgins and Eliza Doolittle reveal their social differences and evolving mutual respect and affection. The subtext in their exchanges helps the audience understand the complexity of their relationship beyond mere words.

Interpreting subtext allows readers and audiences to grasp the true nature of relationships and the characters' emotional states. For instance, in "Who's Afraid of Virginia Woolf?" by Edward Albee, the seemingly casual banter between George and Martha is laden with years of resentment and unfulfilled desires. Understanding the subtext in their dialogue offers a window into their tumultuous marriage and the underlying pain driving their interactions.

To analyse how relationships influence character growth, it's helpful to identify key moments where interactions lead to significant changes in behaviour or perspective. These catalytic moments are often turning points in the narrative. In Lorraine Hansberry's "A Raisin in the Sun," Walter Lee's interactions with his family members, particularly his mother, Lena, lead him to reassess his dreams and responsibilities. The moment he rejects Mr. Lindner's offer illustrates his growth from selfish ambition to a sense of pride and solidarity with his family.

Character Types in Action

Recognising different character types is crucial to understanding and appreciating the depth of a narrative. Characters form the backbone of any drama, and their actions drive the plot forward. Readers who identify various character types in familiar works gain valuable insights into the story's underlying themes and messages. This recognition allows for a deeper context within the narrative, making the experience of reading or watching a drama more immersive and enriching.

For instance, in many popular dramas, you can find distinct character types that help illuminate the storyline. Protagonists often serve as the central figures around which the story revolves. They are usually complex, dynamic characters who grow significantly throughout the narrative. Identifying the protagonist helps readers understand who to root for and follow closely. On the other hand, antagonists function as opposing forces to the protagonists, creating conflict and driving the story forward. Recognising these characters helps readers appreciate the tension and stakes within the plot.

Analysing interactions among different character types further illuminates their contributions to story development. For example, the relationship between a protagonist and an antagonist can reveal much about their motivations and individual traits. In Shakespeare's "Othello," the protagonist and antagonist, Iago, have significantly contrasting motivations and morals, leading to a complex interplay that drives the tragedy forward. Understanding this dynamic engages the audience and enhances critical appreciation of how these characters influence each other's development.

Another essential aspect is recognising typical character tropes in popular dramas. Tropes are standard character types or clichés that recur across various stories, such as the ’tragic hero,‘ the ’comic relief,‘ or the ’wise mentor.‘ While tropes can sometimes seem predictable, they serve as valuable tools for storytelling by providing recognisable patterns for audiences to follow. For instance, in J.K. Rowling’s "Harry Potter" series, Dumbledore fits neatly into the ’wise mentor‘ trope, guiding the protagonist on his journey. Recognising these archetypes can enrich analysis by giving readers a framework to understand character roles and their importance within the story.

Understanding these character types fosters a critical appreciation of character dynamics in storytelling. When readers grasp how different characters interact and affect one another, they begin to see the larger picture of the narrative. For example, in Arthur Miller’s "The Crucible," understanding the character dynamics between John Proctor, Abigail Williams, and Elizabeth Proctor reveals key themes about integrity, love, and redemption. These interactions form the core of the drama and help convey the play’s central message.

When discussing recognising different character types, we must also consider indirect characterisation. Indirect characterisation is when the author shows character traits through actions, thoughts, dialogue, and interactions with other characters. This method requires readers to actively participate in storytelling, as they must infer characteristics and motivations based on subtle cues. For instance, in Harper Lee’s "To Kill a Mockingbird," Scout Finch’s observations and descriptions reveal her father, Atticus Finch’s moral fortitude and compassion without explicitly stating them. By identifying these traits, readers gain a richer understanding of the characters and the overarching themes of racial injustice and moral courage.

In addition to analysing direct and indirect characterisations, looking at how characters contribute to thematic development is beneficial. Thematic development refers to how characters embody and advance the central themes of a drama. Readers can identify how their actions and transformations reflect broader societal issues or philosophical questions by examining characters closely. For example, in Lorraine Hansberry's "A Raisin in the Sun," the struggles of the Younger family portray themes of racial discrimination, economic hardship, and the pursuit of dreams. Each character's journey adds depth to these themes, making the narrative more compelling and thought-provoking.

Moreover, character tropes and their variations offer a rich ground for analysis. While some tropes may seem overused, skilful writers use unique twists to keep the story fresh and engaging. For example, the 'reluctant hero' trope has been present in countless narratives, yet each rendition brings something new. In "The Hobbit" by J.R.R. Tolkien, Bilbo Baggins is initially an unlikely hero, more interested in comfort than adventure. However, his development throughout the story offers a fresh take on the trope, highlighting themes of bravery, personal growth, and the significance of stepping outside one's comfort zone.

Lastly, understanding character arcs—the characters' journeys throughout the narrative—can provide deeper insights into their roles and transformations. Character arcs often involve significant positive, negative, or static changes that reveal essential truths about the characters and their worlds. Observing these changes can enhance readers' engagement by allowing them to witness and reflect on the complexities of human nature. For instance, in George R.R. Martin's "A Song of Ice and Fire" series, the character arc of Jaime Lannister, from a perceived villain to a more nuanced and morally grey character, challenges readers' initial assumptions and encourages more profound engagement with the narrative.

What We Learnt

Throughout this chapter, we have explored the various types of characters that populate dramatic works, including protagonists, antagonists, and foils. By understanding these character roles, readers can better appreciate how characters drive the narrative forward and embody the play's themes. We also delved into characterisation methods, such as direct and indirect techniques, speech patterns, and contrasting and paralleling characters, which are essential for deepening the audience's engagement with the story.

In examining character arcs and transformations, we observed how characters evolve in response to their challenges, highlighting the significance of positive, negative, and static arcs. Additionally, we discussed the impact of relationship dynamics on character development, noting how familial, romantic, and antagonistic interactions shape motivations and growth. Recognising different character types and analysing their roles enhances our critical appreciation of storytelling, providing valuable insights into the intricate mechanisms of drama.

CHAPTER VII

Themes and Symbolism in Drama

Themes and symbolism in drama are essential tools that enable readers to uncover deeper meanings within a play. Examining these elements allows one to comprehend better the underlying messages influencing character development and plot progression. This chapter delves into how themes and symbols enrich dramatic works, encouraging readers to look beyond the surface narrative and engage with the text more profoundly.

This chapter will explore various themes and symbolism in drama. Readers will learn about common themes such as love, betrayal, and identity and how they shape the narratives of famous plays. The chapter will also discuss the significance of cultural contexts that inform these themes, providing insight into historical and societal influences on drama. Additionally, symbols and motifs will be examined, highlighting their role in conveying complex ideas through visual and literary means. Through these discussions, readers will gain valuable tools for interpreting and appreciating dramatic texts more deeply.

Common Themes in Drama

Understanding themes in drama provides readers with a deeper appreciation of a play's narratives and character arcs. This subpoint introduces and explains prevalent themes in dramatic literature, offering a framework for recognising these central ideas when exploring various works by playwrights. Readers can better understand how these elements shape dramatic texts by delving into universal themes, cultural contexts, conflicts, and moral questions.

Universal themes are the backbone of many dramas, transcending time and culture. Themes such as love, betrayal, and identity are omnipresent in dramatic literature. Love, for instance, appears in numerous forms: romantic love, familial love, and even love for one's country or ideals. Shakespeare's "Romeo and Juliet" illustrates the theme of romantic love and its tragic consequences, while Arthur Miller's "The Crucible" explores the destructive power of love intertwined with fanaticism. Similarly, betrayal, a theme often linked with romance, can extend to friendships and allegiances, as seen in plays like "Othello" by Shakespeare, where the protagonist's trust is shattered by deceit. Identity, another central theme, deals with the characters' struggles to understand themselves and their place in the world. In Tennessee Williams' "A Streetcar Named Desire," Blanche DuBois grapples with her fading youth and tarnished reputation, accentuating identity crises and societal expectations. These themes are the foundation for plot and character development, allowing audiences to engage emotionally with the narrative.

Cultural context significantly influences the themes explored in dramatic works, enriching the reading experience and providing depth to thematic relevance. Understanding a play's historical and social background enhances comprehension of its themes. For example, Henrik Ibsen's "A Doll's House" reflects the societal constraints placed on women in 19th-century Norway, critiquing gender roles and marital dynamics. Contextual knowledge about the era allows readers to grasp the significance of Nora's journey toward self-liberation.

Similarly, Lorraine Hansberry's "A Raisin in the Sun" provides insight into the African American experience during the mid-20th century, addressing themes of racial discrimination and the pursuit of the American Dream. Cultural values and historical events shape these narratives, emphasising the play's relevance and guiding readers through a more profound understanding of human experiences across different eras. This contextual awareness bridges the gap between the reader's world and the fictional universe of the play, fostering empathy and a nuanced perspective.

Conflict is a driving force in dramas, propelling narratives and uncovering characters' true ambitions and fears. Internal conflicts, such as personal dilemmas and psychological struggles, reveal characters' innermost thoughts and vulnerabilities. In Sophocles' "Oedipus Rex," the titular character's internal battle with his fate and identity underscores the tragedy of his situation. Such conflicts allow audiences to explore complex human emotions and the characters' ethical difficulties. On the other hand, external conflicts involve societal issues, interpersonal clashes, and confrontations with broader forces. In Arthur Miller's "The Crucible," the mass hysteria and false accusations in Salem reflect the dangers of mob mentality and the clash between individual integrity and societal pressure. Conflicts catalyse character development, pushing individuals to their limits and prompting significant transformations. These elements escalate the tension within the narrative and provide a canvas for exploring broader themes and moral questions.

Moral and ethical questions embedded in dramatic texts provoke philosophical discussions and introspection, inviting readers to reflect on their beliefs and attitudes.

Plays often present scenarios challenging characters' moral compasses, compelling audiences to consider their actions in similar situations. In Bertolt Brecht's "The Caucasian Chalk Circle," the question of rightful ownership versus compassionate stewardship is examined through the story of a peasant girl who protects an abandoned child during a civil war. The ethical dilemma posed encourages viewers to contemplate the nature of justice and responsibility. Similarly, in the existentialist play "Waiting for Godot" by Samuel Beckett, themes of meaningless existence and the human condition prompt audiences to question their purpose and the absurdities of life. Such moral inquiries expand the scope of the drama beyond the stage, engaging readers in a continuous dialogue about human values and societal norms.

Use of Symbols and Motifs

The Role of Symbols and Motifs in Drama

Symbols are crucial elements in drama that convey deeper meanings and enhance the richness of the reading experience. They bridge the surface narrative and the underlying themes of a play, allowing audiences to grasp complex ideas through simple objects, characters, or actions. Consider, for example, the recurring use of a specific colour or object in a dramatic work. A red rose might symbolise love and passion in one context while representing mortality and the fleeting nature of life in another. Using symbols, playwrights can communicate layers of meaning without explicit exposition, encouraging viewers or readers to engage more deeply with the text.

Visual symbols are prominent in many plays, utilising stage design, lighting, costumes, and props to convey symbolic messages. For instance, the use of light and shadow can depict the moral ambiguity of characters or the internal conflicts they face. In Arthur Miller's "The Crucible," the stark lighting and simplicity of the set reflect the severe and oppressive atmosphere of the Salem witch trials, underscoring themes of hysteria and injustice. Similarly, in Tennessee Williams‘ "A Streetcar Named Desire," Blanche DuBois' frequent bathing symbolises her desire to cleanse herself from past sins and guilt. Recognising these visual cues enriches the viewer's understanding and appreciation of the dramatic work.

On the other hand, literary symbols are found within the play's dialogue, actions, and narrative structure. William Shakespeare often employed literary symbols to deepen his audience's engagement with his works. In "Macbeth," the recurring motif of blood represents guilt and the consequences of violent ambition. Lady Macbeth's hallucination of an indelible bloodstain on her hands serves as a powerful symbol of her overwhelming guilt. By identifying and interpreting such symbols, readers can uncover nuanced meanings and thematic significance within the text.

Unlike isolated symbols, Motifs are recurring elements that create cohesion throughout a dramatic work, linking various scenes and characters and evoking specific emotions. These repeated images, phrases, or ideas build a sense of continuity and reinforce the play's central themes. In Henrik Ibsen's "A Doll's House," the dollhouse motif reflects the protagonist Nora's constrained and superficial existence within her marriage. This recurrent imagery emphasises the play's exploration of gender roles and societal expectations. Motifs enhance the emotional resonance of a drama by continually reminding the audience of its core concepts.

Visual and literary symbols span multiple forms, broadening readers' appreciation of artistic elements in drama. Paintings, music, and choreography within a play can serve as visual symbols, enhancing the storytelling and offering new layers of interpretation. Bertolt Brecht's use of music in "Mother Courage and Her Children" provides commentary on the action and character motivations, functioning as both a narrative device and a symbol of resilience amidst adversity. Likewise, in Federico García Lorca's "Blood Wedding," the lyrical and poetic language used by characters transforms everyday dialogue into a mosaic of symbolic expressions, enriching the emotional landscape of the play.

To fully appreciate the depth of symbolism in drama, it is essential to understand techniques for analysing these symbols. Readers can begin by identifying recurring objects, colours, or actions within the text and considering their potential symbolic meanings. Examining the context in which a symbol appears and how it relates to the characters and plot can offer insights into its significance. For instance, in "Death of a Salesman" by Arthur Miller, Willy Loman's seeds symbolise his desire for growth and legacy. Analysing the moments when Willy interacts with the seeds helps reveal his inner turmoil and aspirations.

Another helpful technique is to explore the historical and cultural contexts of the play, as symbols often draw on shared cultural understandings. Recognising references to mythological, religious, or literary traditions can illuminate the symbolic meanings embedded in a dramatic work. For example, the serpent in Oscar Wilde's "Salome" alludes to

Biblical imagery, suggesting themes of temptation and betrayal. Understanding these allusions enables readers to grasp the multifaceted nature of the symbols.

Engaging with critical interpretations and scholarly analyses can also enhance one's comprehension of symbolism in drama. By comparing different viewpoints and exploring various analytical frameworks, readers can develop a more nuanced understanding of the symbolic elements within a play. This process encourages critical thinking and fosters a deeper connection with the text.

Allegory and Metaphor in Dramatic Texts

Allegory and metaphor are potent literary devices frequently employed in drama to offer profound insights and commentary on social issues and human behaviours. These devices transcend the literal meanings of words and scenes, allowing playwrights to weave intricate layers of meaning into their works. Understanding how allegories and metaphors operate within dramatic texts can significantly enhance one's appreciation of a play's more profound messages.

Allegories in famous plays serve as a rich tapestry of meaning, often providing sharp critiques of societal norms. For instance, "Everyman," a medieval morality play, uses the journey of its titular character to reflect on human mortality and the importance of virtuous living. The characters in the play—such as Good Deeds, Knowledge, and Death—are personifications of abstract concepts, creating a symbolic narrative that encourages the audience to reflect on their lives and moral choices.

Similarly, George Orwell's "Animal Farm" is another powerful example of allegory in drama. Through the story of farm animals overthrowing their human farmer only to succumb to tyranny themselves, Orwell critiques the Russian Revolution and the subsequent rise of Soviet totalitarianism. Each character represents historical figures or political ideologies, making the narrative a complex allegory about power, corruption, and betrayal. By engaging with these symbolic elements, readers and audiences can better understand the text and the real-world issues it addresses.

Metaphors, on the other hand, enrich dialogue and character interaction by expressing complex ideas through familiar imagery. In William Shakespeare's "Macbeth," the repeated use of blood as a metaphor helps explore themes of guilt, ambition, and moral corruption. When Lady Macbeth laments, "Out, damned spot! Out, I say!" she is not just speaking about literal bloodstains but also about her overwhelming sense of guilt and complicity in the murders her husband has committed. This metaphorical language allows the audience to grasp the psychological turmoil experienced by the characters, adding depth to their portrayal.

Another excellent example is Arthur Miller's "The Crucible," which uses the metaphor of witch trials to comment on the paranoia and injustice during the McCarthy era in America. The hysteria and accusations that drive the play's plot mirror the real-life political climate of fear and suspicion, making the metaphor resonate strongly with contemporary audiences. Through powerful metaphors, Miller effectively communicates the destructive nature of fanaticism and the consequences of mass hysteria.

To interpret these allegorical and metaphorical designs in dramatic texts, it is helpful to examine the connections between fictional worlds and real-life contexts. A practical approach involves identifying key symbols and characters and exploring what they represent in the broader social or political landscape. For example, in Bertolt Brecht's "Mother Courage and Her Children," Mother Courage symbolises the struggles and contradictions of war profiteering. By analysing her actions and their implications within the Thirty Years' War context, readers can draw parallels to modern conflicts and the ethical dilemmas they present.

Another technique is to study the historical and cultural backdrop against which the play was written. Understanding the socio-political environment of a work like Sophocles' "Antigone" provides insight into why certain characters and themes are depicted as they are. Antigone's defiance against Creon's unjust laws makes more sense when viewed in the context of ancient Greek values regarding family loyalty and divine law versus human law. Drawing these connections helps readers appreciate the layered meanings embedded in the text.

In examining the impact of allegorical and metaphorical elements on audience perception, it becomes clear that these devices foster emotional connections to characters and their journeys. Allegories and metaphors compel viewers to engage with the material intellectually and emotionally. For example, Tony Kushner's "Angels in America" blends realism with supernatural elements, using characters like the angel and Prior's visions to metaphorically address themes of illness, despair, and hope amidst the AIDS crisis. This blend of allegory and reality creates an emotional resonance that makes the play not just a story but a poignant reflection on a critical historical period.

Moreover, metaphors can make abstract concepts more relatable by connecting them to everyday experiences. In Tennessee Williams' "A Streetcar Named Desire," the streetcar is a metaphor for the unstoppable force of desire and fate in Blanche DuBois's life. Her constant references to the streetcar remind the audience of the driving forces behind her actions and ultimate downfall, making her plight both tragic and comprehensible.

Educators and students can benefit significantly from these observations by applying them to their studies and performances. Recognising the allegorical subtexts and metaphorical undertones in dramatic works can open new avenues for analysis and interpretation. For instance, discussing the symbolic aspects of Henrik Ibsen's "A Doll's House" in a classroom can reveal critical perspectives on gender roles and societal expectations. Students examining Nora's journey from a subservient wife to an independent individual can better understand the play's commentary on personal liberation and societal constraints.

Theatre enthusiasts and amateur performers, too, can deepen their craft by recognising how allegories and metaphors shape character motivations and plot developments. By tapping into these deeper meanings, actors can bring a richer, more nuanced performance to the stage. For example, understanding the biblical allegories in T.S. Eliot's "Murder in the Cathedral" allows performers to imbue their roles with a sense of spiritual gravity, enhancing the audience's experience of the play's central themes of martyrdom and redemption.

Interpreting Subtext and Underlying Messages

Subtext, the underlying meaning beneath spoken words, plays a crucial role in drama. It allows audiences to understand what characters truly desire or struggle with beyond their outward expressions. Discerning subtexts will enable readers to engage more deeply with character intentions and the motivations driving plot developments.

To explore how subtext clarifies characters' true desires, consider a scene where a character says one thing but means another. A character's spoken words might often contrast sharply with their internal struggles. For example, a character may express joy but feel deep sorrow. This duality invites audiences to look beyond surface dialogue, uncovering the authentic emotions and intentions that propel the narrative forward. Recognising these layers helps readers grasp why characters behave as they do, fostering a richer appreciation of the storyline.

Analysing scenes with compelling subtext is a powerful tool for understanding deeper insights not overtly stated in dialogue. For instance, take a dramatic exchange between two characters where tension is palpable yet unspoken. The silence pauses, and body language might reveal more about their relationship than any spoken word. Observing these subtleties helps uncover hidden conflicts or alliances that shape the plot. This analytical approach teaches readers to pay attention to what is left unsaid, deepening their engagement with the text.

Effective subtext often relies on nonverbal cues and subtle shifts in interactions. These elements inform relationships and power dynamics within the drama. Imagine a scene where a character's glance or hesitant movement speaks volumes about their attitude toward another character. Such moments can indicate alliances, betrayals, or evolving dynamics. Understanding these nuances enhances the audience's ability to interpret complicated relationships, providing a clearer view of the social structures within the play.

To further appreciate the significance of subtext, consider formulating interpretive questions that dive into character arcs and thematic implications. Questions like "What does this character truly want?" or "How does their internal conflict reflect broader themes?" encourage readers to think critically about the text. Students can develop more nuanced interpretations of characters and plots by addressing these queries. This method of questioning promotes active engagement, allowing readers to connect more deeply with the material.

One guideline for readers is to look for inconsistencies between a character's words and actions. These discrepancies often signal subtextual elements. The subtext may reveal their true intentions in a scene where a character professes loyalty yet acts deceitfully. Identifying such contradictions enables readers to uncover the layered meanings that enrich the dramatic narrative.

Another effective strategy is to observe scenes for pauses and silences. These moments are ripe with subtext, often indicating internal turmoil or unspoken thoughts. For instance, prolonged silence after a significant statement can suggest emotional weight or unresolved tension. By paying attention to these silent beats, readers can gain insights into the characters' inner worlds and the story's complex emotional landscape.

Additionally, analysing body language and facial expressions provides clues to subtext. A character's posture, gestures, and facial cues can communicate more than their lines. Understanding these nonverbal signals helps readers decode the true nature of interactions and the underlying power dynamics at play. When a character avoids eye contact or crosses their arms defensively, it might hint at discomfort or hidden agendas, enriching the audience's comprehension of the scene.

Discussing subtext can lead to more engaging classroom conversations for educators and students. Encouraging students to share their interpretations of subtextual elements fosters a collaborative learning environment. These discussions can help students develop critical thinking skills and a deeper appreciation for the complexities of dramatic texts. Teachers and students can uncover new perspectives and insights by exploring subtext together.

Cultural Context in Drama

Understanding a play's cultural context is crucial for enriching the reading experience and deepening comprehension of its thematic relevance. As an art form, drama reflects the society in which it is created, making awareness of cultural situations and historical moments key to grasping its deeper meanings.

Specific themes in dramas are often directly influenced by the cultural and historical contexts in which they were written. For instance, Arthur Miller's "The Crucible," set during the Salem Witch Trials, can be seen as a response to McCarthyism in the 1950s United States. Understanding the fear and paranoia that characterised both periods allows readers to see how Miller uses themes of hysteria and injustice to comment on his own time. Similarly, William Shakespeare's exploration of power and ambition in "Macbeth" takes on different layers when viewed in Elizabethan England's political climate, emphasising how history shapes dramatic narratives.

Contextual knowledge enables readers to connect personal experiences with dramatic texts, fostering empathy and engagement. Students become more emotionally invested When they recognise parallels between their lives and the worlds depicted in plays. Take Lorraine Hansberry's "A Raisin in the Sun," which delves into systemic racism and dreams deferred. By understanding the racial tensions and the Civil Rights Movement of the 1950s and 60s, readers can better relate to the characters' struggles and aspirations, reflecting on those challenges in contemporary society or their personal lives. This connection makes the themes more poignant and accessible.

Cultural values also shape how themes are interpreted and their significance. Different cultures may emphasise particular aspects of a play's themes based on their unique social norms and values. In Henrik Ibsen's "A Doll's House," the theme of gender roles and female emancipation resonates differently across cultures. While some audiences might focus on Nora's freedom, others might emphasise the societal pressures she faces. Recognising these diverse perspectives helps readers appreciate the multifaceted nature of dramatic works. It discusses how varying cultural backgrounds impact the reception and meaning drawn from the same narrative, expanding the reader's viewpoint beyond a single interpretation.

Moreover, recognising cultural narratives can further shape the thematic discourse within the drama. Plays often incorporate storytelling traditions and motifs prevalent in the writer's culture, which provide insight into human experiences across different societies. For example, August Wilson's "Fences" integrates African American oral tradition and folklore, addressing themes of family and legacy against racial discrimination. Being aware of these cultural narratives not only enriches the understanding of the play's themes but also offers a broader comprehension of the playwright's messages about identity and resistance. It highlights the importance of preserving cultural heritage and provides a window into the collective consciousness of a community.

Examining these elements reveals why cultural context is indispensable for fully appreciating dramatic works. To enhance this understanding further, educators should encourage students to explore the historical and cultural background of the plays they study. This could involve researching the period in which the play was written, understanding the societal issues, and discussing how these factors influence the themes presented. Such an approach fosters a more immersive and informed reading experience.

Recognising these cultural contexts can significantly improve the performances of theatre enthusiasts and performers. Actors bring depth to their characters by understanding the societal forces in their narratives, making their portrayals more authentic and resonant. Directors can make informed decisions about staging and interpretation that align with the cultural and historical nuances of the text, providing audiences with a richer, more engaging theatrical experience.

What We Learnt

This chapter has explored the various themes and symbols in dramatic texts, highlighting their significance in shaping characterisation and narrative. Readers can gain deeper insights into character motivations and plot developments by understanding universal themes like love, betrayal, and identity. Cultural contexts further enrich this understanding, providing a backdrop that clarifies these themes' historical and social influences. Additionally, recognising conflicts and moral questions within plays allows for a comprehensive appreciation of the complex human emotions and ethical dilemmas.

Delving into symbols, motifs, allegories, and metaphors, the chapter emphasised how these literary devices convey deeper meanings beyond the surface narrative. Identifying subtext and underlying messages helps readers uncover characters' true intentions and desires, enhancing engagement with the text. This knowledge is crucial for young adults studying literature, educators guiding students through dramatic works, and theatre enthusiasts seeking to improve their performance skills. Through these analytical tools, readers can develop a more nuanced perspective on the rich layers of meaning embedded in dramatic texts.

CHAPTER VIII

Dialogue and Language in Drama

Dialogue in drama is critical in conveying meaning, advancing the plot, and shaping characters. This chapter delves into the multifaceted functions of dialogue, underscoring its importance in creating engaging and meaningful dramatic works. By examining various aspects such as exposition, character development, plot advancement, and atmosphere creation, readers will better understand how dialogue operates within the drama framework. Through this exploration, the chapter aims to illuminate how spoken language enriches a dramatic narrative.

Throughout the chapter, several vital functions of dialogue are dissected to reveal their contributions to the overall impact of a play. Dialogue for exposition efficiently provides essential background information, making it an indispensable tool for playwrights. Additionally, character development is achieved through distinct speech patterns, word choices, and accents, offering insights into the personalities and transformations of characters. The chapter also explores how dialogue propels the plot by introducing conflicts, resolving issues, and revealing secrets. Lastly, the role of dialogue in setting the mood and creating atmosphere is discussed, demonstrating how carefully crafted words can evoke specific emotions and responses from the audience.

Functions of Dialogue

Dialogue is a fundamental component in drama, essential for conveying information, developing characters, advancing the plot, and creating atmosphere. This section will delve into each function, elucidating how dialogue achieves these aims and enhancing readers' understanding of its multi-faceted role in dramatic texts.

First, let's explore *exposition through dialogue*. Dialogue often serves as a tool for providing background information that might otherwise require lengthy narration. In plays with limited time and space, dialogue offers an efficient way to introduce critical details about the setting, characters, and situations. For instance, a character might reveal past events during a conversation rather than using a narrator or elaborate stage directions. In Arthur Miller's "The Crucible", early dialogues between characters like Reverend Parris and Abigail Williams quickly introduce the audience to the town's tensions and history of witch trials. This technique keeps the audience engaged while seamlessly integrating exposition into the storyline.

Guideline: When incorporating exposition into dialogue, ensure it feels natural and doesn't overload the audience with information. Characters should have realistic reasons for revealing background details, maintaining a flow that aligns with their motivations and the narrative context.

Another vital function of dialogue is in *character development*. Each character's unique way of speaking contributes significantly to their identity and helps distinguish them from one another. Their choice of words, speech patterns, and even accents provide insights into their backgrounds, personalities, and emotions. William Shakespeare was a master of using dialogue for character development. In "Hamlet," the protagonist's introspective and philosophical dialogues contrast sharply with the more straightforward and sometimes crude speech of characters like Polonius, Rosencrantz, and Guildenstern, highlighting Hamlet's inner turmoil and intellectual nature. A character's language can also evolve, reflecting their personal growth or changes in their circumstances throughout the play.

For example, consider Eliza Doolittle's transformation in George Bernard Shaw's "Pygmalion." Her shift from a thick Cockney accent to refined speech symbolises her journey from a flower girl to a lady, marking significant character development achieved through dialogue. Observing their speech allows Audiences to gain deeper insights into characters' traits and transformations.

Next, we examine how dialogue is crucial in *advancing the plot*. Conversations between characters can lead to pivotal plot points and turning events. A dialogue exchange can introduce conflict, resolve issues, reveal secrets, or propel characters into new situations. In Tennessee Williams's "A Streetcar Named Desire," the escalating tension between Blanche DuBois and Stanley Kowalski is articulated through sharp and confrontational dialogue. As they verbally spar, the underlying conflicts emerge, driving the story towards its climax. Effective dialogue reveals what is happening and why it matters, ensuring that each line spoken has a purpose in moving the narrative forward.

Additionally, *creating atmosphere* is another critical function of dialogue in drama. The playwright's choice of words can evoke various emotions and set the tone for scenes, influencing the audience's emotional response. Language can create a sense of tension, humour, sadness, or any other mood that the scene requires. Consider the menacing atmosphere created by the witches' cryptic dialogue in Shakespeare's "Macbeth" opening scene. Their eerie chant of "Fair is foul, and foul is fair" immediately sets a tone of ambiguity and foreboding, hinting at the following dark events. Conversely, in a comedic play like Oscar Wilde's "The Importance of Being Earnest", witty dialogue creates a light-hearted and entertaining atmosphere.

Subtext and Implication

When exploring the more profound truths revealed through dialogue in drama, it is essential to grasp the concept of subtext. Subtext refers to the underlying messages or meanings not explicitly spoken by characters but implied beneath their words. This communication layer can give audiences insights into a character's true feelings, intentions, and motivations.

To illustrate this, consider a scene where a character says they're "fine" when their body language suggests otherwise. Despite the spoken words indicating well-being, the subtext reveals emotional turmoil or distress. Writers use subtext to convey complex emotional states and internal conflicts without outright stating them, creating more affluent, nuanced characters and situations.

Understanding subtext requires careful attention to context and nonverbal cues such as tone, facial expressions, and gestures. For instance, in Arthur Miller's play The Crucible, much of the tension between John Proctor and Abigail Williams stems from subtext. When they engage in seemingly innocent dialogue, the subtext of past indiscretions and unresolved feelings adds a charged undercurrent to their exchanges. Audiences can discern the more profound significance of their interactions by reading between the lines, which may be pivotal to the storyline.

Another crucial aspect of dialogue in drama is the role of silence. Often, what a character does not say can be just as impactful as what they do say. Strategic pauses, hesitations, and moments of silence can communicate emotions ranging from fear and uncertainty to defiance and contemplation. Silence lets characters verbally articulate what is too difficult or dangerous to speak, deepening the narrative.

Shakespeare masterfully employs silence in many of his plays. For example, in "Hamlet," Ophelia's silence during her exchanges with Hamlet speaks volumes. Her lack of verbal response conveys her internal struggle and the oppressive societal constraints placed upon her. Similarly, in Harold Pinter's works, known for the “Pinter pause,” silence creates an atmosphere of tension and ambiguity, forcing the audience to infer meaning and intention from the lack of dialogue.

Irony in dialogue is a powerful tool for revealing deeper thematic elements and character intentions. Irony occurs when characters say something contrasting with what they truly mean or believe. Depending on the context, this can create layers of meaning and add complexity to the narrative, often leading to dramatic or comedic effects.

For example, in Oscar Wilde's "The Importance of Being Earnest," the characters frequently engage in ironic dialogue highlighting social conventions‘ absurdities. When Algernon casually remarks, "The truth is rarely pure and never simple," he ironically underscores the entangled deceptions within the play. Such use of irony not only entertains but also prompts audiences to question societal norms and the sincerity of human relationships.

Irony can also heighten tension and conflict within a story. Consider the character of Iago in Shakespeare's "Othello." Iago manipulates Othello into doubting Desdemona's fidelity through ironic statements and duplicity, stirring a destructive jealousy. The audience, aware of Iago's true intentions, witnesses the tragic consequences of Othello misinterpreting the layered meanings in Iago's dialogue. This brings us to how conflict through dialogue drives pivotal scenes in drama.

Conflict is often the heartbeat of dramatic narratives, and dialogue is a primary vehicle for expressing and escalating this conflict. When characters exchange words loaded with subtext, irony, or unspoken tension, their interactions become battlegrounds of conflicting desires, values, and emotions. Such dialogue propels the plot and reveals crucial aspects of character psychology and themes.

In Tennessee Williams's "A Streetcar Named Desire," the heated dialogues between Blanche DuBois and Stanley Kowalski epitomise conflict through dialogue. Their conversations are fraught with subtextual battles over power, truth, and survival. Each line they deliver is imbued with hidden meanings and implications, gradually unravelling their vulnerabilities and driving the narrative towards its dramatic climax.

To analyse these dynamics effectively, it is helpful to pay close attention to how characters' words align or clash with their actions and the broader context of the play. Consider how their language, tone, and timing choices build tension and advance conflict. Evaluating key scenes where dialogue becomes a battlefield can offer deep insights into the characters' inner workings and the piece's overall message.

Language Styles Across Different Periods

The evolution of language in drama provides an insightful lens through which to examine how characters and themes are developed and conveyed over time. Understanding this evolution helps us appreciate the shifts in societal norms, artistic expression, and cultural influences reflected in dramatic works across different periods.

Classical Language

The language is characterised by its formal and elevated style in ancient dramas, such as those from Greek and Roman theatre. This choice was not merely a stylistic one but served a functional purpose. The splendid and poetic diction highlighted the nobility and gravitas of the characters, often gods, heroes, or royalty, whose lofty speech matched their larger-than-life roles and moral struggles. For example, in plays like Sophocles' "Oedipus Rex," the complex language expresses profound philosophical and ethical dilemmas, enhancing the audience's perception of the tragic hero's fate.

Similarly, the use of verse, particularly iambic pentameter, contributed to this heightened sense of drama and importance. The structure and rhythm of the language were crucial in helping actors memorise lines and audiences follow the plot. Furthermore, this stylised speech facilitated the projection of voices in large arenas, ensuring that even spectators seated far from the stage could hear and understand the dialogue.

Shakespearean Language

Moving into the Elizabethan era, we observe a shift in the complexity and creativity of dramatic language exemplified by William Shakespeare. Shakespeare's works are renowned for their intricate wordplay, inventive vocabulary, and poetic devices like metaphor, simile, and alliteration. His unique language choices were instrumental in conveying complex human emotions and psychological depth. For instance, Hamlet's famous soliloquy, "To be or not to be," delves into existential angst and moral uncertainty through its rich and layered use of language.

Additionally, Shakespeare's manipulation of language extended beyond individual speeches to include conversational dynamics between characters. The rapid exchange of witty banter in comedies like "Much Ado About Nothing" reveals social hierarchies and personal relationships. At the same time, the lofty and formal language in his tragedies underscores themes of honour, fate, and downfall. Shakespeare's innovative use of language also allowed him to create new words and phrases, many of which have become integral to the English lexicon.

Modern Language Styles

In the 20th century, they ushered in a significant transformation in the language of drama, reflecting broader social changes and technological advancements. Modern playwrights began to favour more informal, realistic, and conversational speech, aiming to depict everyday life and ordinary people more accurately. This shift towards naturalism can be seen in the works of playwrights like Arthur Miller and Tennessee Williams.

For example, in Miller's "Death of a Salesman," the language mirrors the mundane and often fragmented nature of the protagonist Willy Loman's thoughts and speech, emphasising his disillusionment and mental decline. Similarly, Tennessee Williams' "A Streetcar Named Desire" employs colloquial language to highlight its characters' gritty, raw emotions and strained interactions. This period also saw the emergence of diverse voices and dialects on stage, reflecting the multicultural fabric of contemporary society.

Moreover, modern drama often incorporates vernacular speech, idiomatic expressions, and regional dialects to enhance authenticity and relatability. This trend reflects a democratisation of theatre, where the experiences and voices of marginalised communities are given prominence, challenging traditional narratives and power structures.

Global Perspectives

Expanding our view beyond Western traditions, we must recognise non-Western dramas' diverse and rich linguistic heritage. Languages used in various global theatres offer unique insights into their respective cultures and societal values. For instance, traditional Japanese Noh theatre employs a highly stylised and symbolic language that, while archaic, conveys spiritual and metaphysical themes. The minimalist and ritualistic dialogue harmonises with the controlled movements and expressions of the performers, creating a meditative atmosphere.

In Indian classical theatre, especially in Sanskrit drama like Kalidasa's "Shakuntala," the language is infused with lyrical beauty and vivid imagery, drawing from ancient epics and religious texts. The dialogues are crafted to evoke emotional resonance and convey moral and philosophical teachings, often intertwining narrative and didactic purposes.

African drama, particularly in post-colonial contexts, often blends indigenous and colonial languages, resulting in a hybrid linguistic style that reflects the complexities of identity, resistance, and cultural reclamation. Wole Soyinka's plays, for instance, integrate Yoruba proverbs, chants, and songs, enriching the narrative with layers of cultural significance and historical memory.

Latin American drama presents another fascinating case. Playwrights like Federico García Lorca use poetic and folkloric elements within Spanish to explore themes of love, oppression, and social justice. The linguistic richness of these dramas provides a window into Latin American societies‘ unique mythologies and historical experiences.

Impact of Monologues and Soliloquies

Monologues and soliloquies are essential to dramatic works and powerful tools for character introspection and narrative advancement. These forms of dialogue enrich the audience's understanding of a character's inner world and help drive the story forward. While they may seem similar on the surface, each has a distinct purpose and impact on drama.

Understanding monologues involves recognising their unique role in revealing individual perspectives. Unlike dialogues, where multiple characters interact, monologues allow one character to express their thoughts and feelings uninterrupted. This uninterrupted speech provides deep insight into the character's motivations, desires, and conflicts. This can be particularly enlightening for young literature students as it helps them develop a more nuanced understanding of each character's role within the narrative.

In plays like Tennessee Williams' "A Streetcar Named Desire," Blanche Dubois' monologues provide profound insights into her troubled past and deteriorating mental state, making her actions and decisions throughout the play more understandable.

Soliloquy, on the other hand, is a specific type of monologue used primarily for introspection. When a character delivers a monologue, they are typically alone on stage, directly addressing themselves or the audience. This creates a sense of intimacy, allowing the audience to glimpse the character's true self, unfiltered by interactions with others. Shakespeare's works offer some of the most famous examples of soliloquies. In "Hamlet," the titular character's "To be or not to be" soliloquy reveals his deep existential angst and contemplation of life and death. This moment of introspection informs the audience about Hamlet's internal struggle and adds emotional depth to the narrative, making his subsequent actions more impactful.

Dramatic tension is another crucial aspect generated through monologues and soliloquies. These speeches often occur at pivotal moments in the plot, where a character's internal conflict climaxes. During these moments, the audience gains insight into the stakes and possible consequences of the character's decisions. In Arthur Miller's "Death of a Salesman," Willy Loman's monologues reveal his desperate need for success and validation, heightening the dramatic tension as his life's unravelling becomes inevitable. The audience feels the weight of Willy's dreams and the impending tragedy, making the final act all the more moving.

The performance aspect of monologues and soliloquies cannot be understated. An actor's interpretation of these speeches can significantly influence the audience's perception of the character and the overall narrative. Experienced actors bring out the nuanced emotions behind the text, using their voice, facial expressions, and body language to convey the character's inner turmoil or joy. For instance, an actor portraying Lady Macbeth in Shakespeare's "Macbeth" might use a trembling voice and frantic gestures during her "Out, damned spot!" soliloquy to emphasise her growing guilt and madness. Educators can guide students to analyse different performances of the same monologue to understand how various interpretations can alter the audience's engagement with the character and the story.

The Art of Crafting Effective Dialogue

One must first understand the balance between naturalism and stylisation to provide techniques and insights for writing compelling and authentic dialogue in drama. Naturalistic dialogue aims to mirror everyday speech, offering authenticity and relatability. This approach helps audiences feel connected to characters and their stories. However, too much realism can lead to mundane or incoherent exchanges that may bog down the narrative's pacing.

Stylisation, on the other hand, embraces more artistic expressions of language. It allows playwrights to infuse dialogue with heightened emotions, poetic devices, and unique linguistic elements that captivate audiences. The key is finding a balance that serves the story and its characters. For example, Tennessee Williams often blended naturalistic dialogue with lyrical monologues in his plays, creating a rich tapestry of realism and stylised emotion. By observing how renowned playwrights balance these methods, aspiring writers can craft believable and artistically engaging dialogue.

Enhancing authenticity in dialogue involves using dialects and colloquialisms that reflect a character's background and culture. Dialects can reveal much about a character's origin, education level, and social status. Mark Twain's use of regional dialects in "The Adventures of Huckleberry Finn" is a notable example of this technique. It immerses readers in the setting while giving each character a distinctive voice.

However, writers must use dialects and colloquialisms judiciously. Overuse can render dialogue unintelligible or perpetuate stereotypes. The goal is to enhance believability without compromising clarity. Researching regional speech patterns and listening to people from various backgrounds can provide valuable insight into crafting authentic dialogue. Including occasional idiomatic expressions or slang words can add depth to characters without overwhelming the reader.

Pacing and rhythm are crucial in shaping effective dialogue. Good dialogue has a natural flow that mirrors real-life conversation but also serves the dramatic needs of the scene. The tempo of exchanges can convey urgency, build tension, or create a sense of calm. Rapid-fire dialogue may be used in moments of conflict or high stakes, whereas slower, measured dialogue might suit reflective or intimate scenes.

In drama, timing often plays a pivotal role. A well-placed pause or interruption can heighten emotional impact or reveal underlying character tensions. For instance, Harold Pinter's dialogues are famous for their strategic pauses, which create a palpable sense of unease and uncertainty. Understanding when to accelerate or decelerate the pace can significantly affect how the audience perceives a scene.

Rewriting and refining dialogue is essential to ensure clarity and enhance impact. Initial drafts of dialogue often contain unnecessary repetition, unnatural phrasing, or irrelevant details. During revision, writers should focus on distilling dialogue to its most potent form. Eliminating extraneous words and sharpening exchanges will make the dialogue more dynamic and engaging.

Reading dialogue aloud is an invaluable tool in this process. Hearing the words helps identify awkward phrasing or stilted rhythms that may not appear on the page. Additionally, having others act out scenes can provide insight into how the dialogue flows and whether it conveys the intended emotions and subtext. Feedback from actors or peers can highlight areas for improvement that the writer may have overlooked.

Writers should also consider the visual aspect of dialogue in a script. Formatting can influence how dialogue is read and interpreted. Clear demarcations of pauses, beats, and stage directions help guide performers in delivering dialogue effectively. Ensuring that each line serves a purpose—whether it drives the plot, reveals character, or creates atmosphere—is paramount.

What We Learnt

In this chapter, we explored the powerful role of spoken language in drama. We examined how dialogue serves multiple crucial functions: conveying essential background information through exposition, developing characters by revealing their unique speech patterns and evolving language, advancing the plot through pivotal exchanges, and creating an atmosphere with carefully chosen words that set the scene's tone. Through examples from notable works like Miller's "The Crucible" and Shakespeare's plays, we saw how effective dialogue integrates critical details, enhances character development, drives narratives forward, and evokes emotional responses.

Moreover, we delved into the importance of subtext, irony, and the strategic use of silence in adding layers of meaning to dialogue. Understanding these subtleties allows readers to gain deeper insights into the character's feelings and motivations. We also highlighted the varied language styles across different periods and cultures, demonstrating how they reflect societal changes and artistic expression. As young adults, educators, and theatre enthusiasts engage with these dramatic techniques, they can develop a richer appreciation of plays and improve their analytical and performance skills.

CHAPTER IX

Staging and Performance

Staging and performance bridge the written script and the live theatrical experience. When a play transitions from page to stage, it undergoes a transformative process involving visual, auditory, and kinesthetic elements. These elements work together to bring the narrative to life in a manner that engages the audience's senses and emotions more deeply than the text alone can.

This chapter will explore various artistic components contributing to effective staging and performance. We will examine the pivotal role of the director in shaping the production, including their vision, casting choices, and collaboration with the creative team. Additionally, we will delve into the significance of set design and props in creating an immersive environment and how costumes and makeup enhance character portrayal and thematic representation. Lastly, we will investigate the impact of lighting and sound effects on mood, atmosphere, and strategies for maintaining audience engagement and pacing throughout a performance. Through these discussions, readers will understand how drama transcends the written word, coming alive on stage to captivate and move its audience.

Role of the Director

In theatre arts, the director is a pivotal figure who shapes the overall production. A director's influence extends beyond simply rehearsing scenes with actors; it encompasses creating an artistic vision that brings the script to life and resonates deeply with the performers and the audience.

The first step in a director's journey is to develop a vision and interpretation of the play. This process involves delving into the script to uncover its themes, undertones, and emotional arcs. The director must decide how these elements will be represented on stage, considering tone, pacing, and visual style. For instance, in Shakespeare's "Hamlet," a director might opt for a traditional Elizabethan setting or a modern, contemporary backdrop, offering a unique perspective on the timeless narrative.

Casting decisions are another critical aspect where the director's choices can significantly influence the dynamics and chemistry on stage. The right cast can bring characters to life in powerful and unexpected ways, while poor casting can lead to a disjointed performance. A director must have a keen eye for talent and understand how different actors' strengths and styles will mesh together. For example, casting an actor known for their emotional depth in the role of Hamlet can bring new layers of intensity and vulnerability to the character, thereby enriching the audience's experience.

Collaboration with the creative team is essential for realising the director's vision. This team typically includes set, costume, and lighting designers, each contributing their expertise to create a cohesive and immersive world on stage. The director must communicate their vision clearly and work closely with these artists to ensure that every element aligns with the intended interpretation of the play. The set design, for instance, must reflect the time and place and enhance the story's thematic underpinnings. Similarly, costumes should help define the characters and their relationships, while lighting can be used to evoke specific moods and highlight important moments.

Audience engagement is another crucial consideration for directors. A successful performance not only conveys the story but also connects with the audience on an emotional level. Directors must think about how to use staging, pacing, and actors' interactions to keep the audience invested from start to finish. They might employ techniques like breaking the fourth wall, where actors address the audience directly, or using innovative staging that allows for a more immersive experience. In productions like "Our Town" by Thornton Wilder, minimalistic sets and direct audience engagement underline the play's themes of community and the passage of time, making the audience feel like active participants in the narrative.

A guideline is to ensure the cast's performances align with the director's vision. This involves thorough rehearsals and constant communication between the director and the actors. The goal is to maintain consistency in tone and style, ensuring that every performance element contributes to the overall vision. Through workshops and feedback sessions, directors can fine-tune performances, encouraging actors to explore their characters profoundly and understand their motivations. This collaborative process helps create a more nuanced and compelling portrayal that resonates with the audience.

Directors often navigate different directorial styles, ranging from auteur approaches, where the director's style and vision dominate, to more collaborative frameworks that emphasise the entire creative team's input. Each style offers unique advantages and challenges. An auteur director might bring a robust and distinctive vision to the play, potentially offering fresh interpretations and daring innovations. Conversely, a collaborative approach might foster a more inclusive environment, allowing diverse perspectives and ideas to shape the final production.

Examples of notable directors can illustrate the impact of various directing styles. Directors like Peter Brook and Anne Bogart have pushed the boundaries of traditional theatre, introducing innovative techniques and philosophies that have reshaped modern theatre practices. Their work inspires and is a benchmark for aspiring directors, demonstrating the transformative power of a well-executed vision.

Set Design and Props

In theatre, set design and props are indispensable components that breathe life into a dramatic piece. They create a tangible world where stories unfold, immersing the audience in the play's atmosphere and context. This section delves into how these elements contribute to storytelling, balancing artistic vision with practical production considerations.

Creating the Environment: Set design plays a pivotal role in establishing the environment of a play, offering visual cues that reflect the themes and setting. For instance, a meticulously crafted Victorian parlour set immediately transports the audience to 19th-century England, grounding them in the historical and social context of the drama. The design conveys not just the physical space but also the mood and tone of the narrative. Designers often employ colour schemes, architectural styles, and spatial arrangements to evoke specific emotions—the bleakness of a dystopian future or the elegance of a royal court. The environment becomes a silent yet powerful storyteller, enhancing the audience's connection to the unfolding action.

Functionality of Props: Beyond their decorative appeal, props are essential tools that advance the plot and illuminate character relationships. A simple object like a locket can become a poignant symbol of lost love or hidden secrets, carrying significant narrative weight. Props provide actors with tangible items to interact with, fostering a deeper embodiment of their roles. Consider Shakespeare's "Hamlet" and the iconic skull in the graveyard scene. This prop adds visual interest and catalyses Hamlet's introspection on mortality and human existence. Through thoughtful selection and placement, props can transform from objects into critical storytelling devices that enrich the tapestry.

Budget and Practicality: While the artistic vision for set design and props is vital, it must be balanced against budgetary constraints and practical considerations. Theatre productions often work within limited financial resources, necessitating creative solutions to achieve desired effects without exceeding allocated funds. For example, a community theatre might use painted backdrops and cleverly repurposed furniture to suggest opulent settings without the expense of elaborate constructions. Effective budgeting requires collaboration among designers, directors, and production teams to prioritise elements that most significantly impact the storytelling. This balance ensures that the artistic integrity of the performance is maintained while adhering to financial realities.

Scene Changes and Movement: An often-overlooked aspect of set design is its ability to accommodate scene changes and facilitate smooth transitions. Plays frequently involve shifts in location or time, requiring flexible sets that can be quickly and quietly altered. Innovative designs might include modular pieces that can be rearranged or multi-purpose structures that serve different functions in various scenes. Additionally, the set must support the play's pacing, allowing for dynamic movement and interaction among the cast. Seamless transitions maintain the flow of the narrative, preventing disruptions that could disengage the audience. Effective set design marries aesthetics with functionality, ensuring that each element serves the dual purpose of enhancing the visual experience and supporting the practical demands of live performance.

Costumes and Makeup

Costumes and makeup transform written characters into vivid, believable individuals on stage. Beyond the script, these visual elements play a pivotal role in character development, enabling actors to embody their roles fully and allowing audiences to grasp critical themes and narratives visually.

Firstly, the identity of each character is brought to life through costumes. The attire worn by an actor can provide immediate insights into who the character is, what they value, and their social status. For instance, a wealthy character might don lavish fabrics like silk or velvet adorned with intricate embellishments, signalling their affluence and power without a word being spoken. Conversely, a lower social stratum character might wear simpler, perhaps even tattered clothing, hinting at their struggles and resilience. These sartorial choices help set the stage for the story, giving the audience cues about the characters' backgrounds and motivations right from their first appearance.

In many plays, costumes are also essential in reflecting the underlying themes. They serve as visual metaphors that resonate with the narrative's core ideas. For example, in a play dealing with themes of freedom and constraint, characters might start in restrictive clothing that gradually becomes looser as they gain independence. This visual storytelling complements the dialogue and actions, creating a cohesive artistic expression that deepens the audience's understanding of the thematic content.

Makeup, similarly, functions as a crucial tool for storytelling. It enhances an actor's portrayal by adding layers of nuance and realism to their performance. Makeup can age a young actor, making them believable as an elderly character, or transform a modern individual into one from a different historical period. Beyond physical transformations, makeup can also signify internal states or mythical aspects. For example, exaggerated or stylised makeup might portray a character's descent into madness or emphasise their role as a mythical creature. Such use of makeup not only adds depth to the character but also maintains the suspension of disbelief necessary for a successful performance.

The process of designing and applying costumes and makeup is highly collaborative. Directors, costume designers, and actors must work closely together to ensure that the visual representation aligns with the overall vision of the play. Directors provide the conceptual framework, guiding the thematic and aesthetic direction. Costume designers translate this vision into tangible designs, considering practicality and artistic expression. Actors then bring these designs to life, allowing the costumes and makeup to inform their movements and interactions on stage. This iterative process ensures that every element works harmoniously, contributing to a unified and compelling production.

For a practical example, consider Shakespeare's "Romeo and Juliet." The costumes in various productions often reflect the conflicting families' wealth and societal status. The Capulet's and Montague's elaborate and richly textured garments highlight their noble standing while showcasing their rivalry through distinct colour palettes. Romeo's transformation from a lovesick youth in sombre attire to a vibrant lover clothed in brighter hues as he embraces his love for Juliet visually narrates his character arc. The makeup used to depict the lovers' tragic end with pale faces and bruised features adds to the poignant final scenes, emphasising the themes of love and loss.

Technological advancements have also influenced costume and makeup design in contemporary theatre. Modern materials and techniques allow for more dynamic and versatile designs that adapt to different settings and interpretations. For example, LED lights integrated into costumes can create stunning visual effects that align with a futuristic or fantastical theme. Similarly, prosthetics and advanced makeup techniques enable more realistic and complex transformations, broadening the scope of characters that can be convincingly portrayed on stage.

While costumes and makeup significantly enhance character development and thematic representation, they also require meticulous planning and execution. Each piece of costume and every brushstroke of makeup must align with the director's vision and the narrative's demands. This level of detail ensures that the audience is transported into the story when the curtains rise, fully immersed in the world created on stage.

Moreover, the effectiveness of costumes and makeup depends on their adaptability throughout the performance. Quick changes between scenes necessitate designs that can be easily altered without sacrificing quality or believability. This aspect is particularly crucial in plays with numerous characters or complex storylines, where seamless transitions maintain the flow and continuity of the production.

Understanding the role of costumes and makeup in educational settings offers students valuable insights into the comprehensive nature of theatrical productions. For drama students, experimenting with costume and makeup design as part of their projects can deepen their appreciation of how these elements contribute to storytelling. They learn to think critically about how visual aspects influence an audience's perception and emotional response, fostering a holistic approach to drama education.

Teachers can use this knowledge to create engaging lesson plans involving practical costume and makeup design exercises. Educators can enhance their interpretative skills and creativity by encouraging students to analyse characters from a visual perspective. Discussions about historical costume styles, cultural influences, and the symbolism behind specific designs can lead to richer, more informed analyses of dramatic works.

Theatre enthusiasts and amateur performers can elevate their appreciation and performance skills by delving into the intricacies of costume and makeup design. Understanding the nuances of these visual tools enables them to make more informed choices in their portrayals, resulting in more compelling and authentic performances. As they experiment with different looks and styles, they gain a deeper connection to their characters and greater confidence on stage.

Lighting and Sound Effects

Lighting and sound effects are fundamental components that intertwine with the narrative of a performance to create an immersive experience for the audience. Through these elements, performances can evoke powerful emotions, set the scene's tone, and guide the audience's reactions in a way that mere dialogue cannot achieve.

Firstly, lighting plays a crucial role in setting the mood of each scene. The manipulation of light intensity, colour, and direction contributes significantly to the emotional tone. For instance, dim lighting with cool blue hues may suggest a sad or mysterious atmosphere, whereas bright lights with warm tones can evoke joy and warmth. Examples from notable productions, such as the use of stark, contrasting lights in "A Streetcar Named Desire," demonstrate how lighting establishes tensions and enhances character interactions. By aligning the lighting design with the narrative's emotional undertones, directors can subtly influence how scenes are perceived by the audience, guiding their emotional journey through the play.

On the other hand, sound effects construct acoustic landscapes that deepen the audience's immersion into the story. Background sounds, like the gentle rustling of leaves or distant urban noises, set the environmental context, making the scene more believable and relatable. Music, whether diegetic (originating within the scene) or non-diegetic (background score), also plays a pivotal role in heightening emotions and signalling shifts in mood. For example, suspenseful music can build anticipation before a critical moment, while soft, melodic tunes might underline the tenderness of a romantic scene. Adequate sound complements the visual elements and enriches the storytelling by engaging the audience's auditory senses.

The synchronisation of sound and lighting with the action on stage is another vital aspect that enhances narrative continuity. This integration ensures that every technical element supports the unfolding drama, creating a seamless experience for the viewer. For instance, a sudden blackout accompanied by a sharp sound effect can signify a dramatic transition or the climax of a scene. In Shakespeare's "Macbeth," thunder and lightning create an ominous atmosphere during the witches' scenes, synchronising natural elements with supernatural occurrences in the plot. Such precise alignment between technical components and on-stage action strengthens the narrative flow and keeps the audience engaged, ensuring they remain attuned to the story's progression.

Modern technology has also significantly transformed lighting and sound design, encouraging experimentation and innovation. Advanced lighting systems, such as LED fixtures and digital projectors, offer designers greater flexibility and control over the visual aspects of a production. These technologies enable the creation of dynamic lighting effects that can rapidly change colours, patterns, and intensities, thus opening new possibilities for visually representing complex emotions and themes. Similarly, advancements in sound engineering, including surround sound setups and sophisticated audio processing software, allow for a more nuanced and layered auditory experience. These tools help designers craft intricate soundscapes that can simulate real-world environments or abstract, fantastical settings, thereby expanding the creative boundaries of theatrical production.

Moreover, interactive lighting and sound installations can actively involve the audience, making the experience more participatory. For example, some productions utilise motion-tracking technology to adjust lighting and sound based on audience movement, creating a sense of unpredictability and engagement. Experimental theatre groups have explored these techniques to break conventional staging norms, providing audiences with a unique, immersive experience that blurs the lines between performer and spectator.

It's also important to consider the collaborative nature of incorporating lighting and sound into a performance. Designers work closely with directors, actors, and other creative team members to ensure that these elements align with the overall vision of the production. This collaboration is essential in achieving coherence and enhancing the impact of storytelling. For instance, discussions between the lighting designer and the costume designer can result in coordinated colour schemes highlighting thematic elements or character development. Similarly, sound designers may consult with the director to determine key moments where audio cues can amplify the narrative's emotional intensity.

Audience Engagement and Pacing

Directors and their creative teams are critical in ensuring a performance captures and retains the audience's attention. They employ various strategies to maintain engagement throughout the play. One fundamental strategy is establishing a strong opening scene that immediately immerses the audience in the story. A compelling start can set the tone for the performance, drawing viewers in with intriguing characters, conflicts, or visually arresting stage setups. As the play progresses, transitions between scenes are meticulously planned to avoid disjointedness that might break the audience's immersion. Seamless scene changes maintain the narrative's flow, keeping the audience captivated.

Another vital approach includes leveraging emotional highs and lows within the story. Directors often orchestrate moments of tension followed by relief, laughter after sadness, or quiet introspection following dramatic events. These emotional shifts prevent monotony and keep the audience emotionally invested. In addition to these narrative techniques, directors may use visual elements such as dynamic lighting, imaginative set designs, and striking costumes to hold the audience's interest.

Moreover, directors utilise techniques that foster direct engagement to break down barriers between the stage and the audience. For instance, breaking the fourth wall—a theatre convention where actors acknowledge the audience—can create an intimate and immersive experience. This technique encourages viewers to feel like participants rather than passive observers. Interactive elements, such as actors moving through the aisles or engaging in direct dialogue with the audience, further enhance this sense of involvement. These approaches make the performance more vivid and memorable, deepening the audience's emotional connection to the story and characters.

The importance of pacing and timing in sustaining audience interest cannot be overstated. Pacing involves managing the speed and rhythm at which the story unfolds. A well-paced performance balances rapid sequences with slower, contemplative moments, thus preventing viewer fatigue. Directors often fine-tune the timing of line deliveries, actions, and scene changes during rehearsals to ensure effective pacing. For example, comedic plays require precise timing to maximise the humour of punchlines, while dramatic performances rely on strategic pauses to heighten tension and reflection.

Furthermore, directors must adapt performances based on audience feedback and reactions. Live theatre offers the unique advantage of real-time audience interaction, allowing directors to observe which aspects resonate most strongly. During previews and early performances, directors might note audience responses to pacing, emotional beats, and engagement tactics. They can then make adjustments, such as altering the timing of specific scenes or modifying interactive elements, to enhance the production's overall impact.

What We Learnt

This chapter has delved into the intricate ways drama transcends mere text and emerges vividly on stage through various artistic components. By examining the role of directors, set design, costumes, makeup, lighting, sound effects, and audience engagement, we see how each element contributes to a cohesive and immersive theatrical experience. Directors shape the vision, ensuring that every part of the production aligns with the narrative's emotional and thematic arcs. Meanwhile, set design and props craft the tangible world of the play, providing context and enhancing storytelling.

Costumes and makeup bring characters to life, offering immediate visual cues about their identities and underlying themes. Lighting and sound effects deepen the audience's immersion by setting the scene's tone and guiding emotional responses. Finally, effective pacing and direct engagement techniques ensure that the audience remains captivated from beginning to end. Together, these elements work harmoniously to transform written drama into a dynamic performance that resonates emotionally and intellectually with its audience.

CHAPTER X

Analysing Historical Context

Analysing historical context is an essential aspect of understanding dramatic works. The political, social, economic, and cultural environments in which a play was written and performed profoundly impact its themes, characters, and reception. By delving into the historical backdrop of a drama, readers and viewers can gain deeper insights into the playwright's intentions and the work's broader societal implications.

This chapter will explore various influences on dramatic narratives, such as political climates and social movements, using examples like Arthur Miller's "The Crucible" and Lorraine Hansberry's "A Raisin in the Sun." It will also discuss how censorship has shaped the content and expression of plays throughout history, referencing Shakespeare and modern-day instances. Additionally, the chapter will examine the role of cultural identity and clashes within dramatic works, considering how these elements contribute to the richness and complexity of character portrayals and storylines. Readers will learn to appreciate the intricate connections between historical context and dramatic art through this analysis, enhancing their interpretation and critical engagement with dramatic texts.

Political and Social Influences

Political climates and social movements profoundly shape dramatic narratives and character behaviour, providing a rich context for understanding the content of plays. Historical dramas often reflect or critique governmental actions and policies, a prime example being Arthur Miller's 'The Crucible'. Written during the height of McCarthyism in the 1950s, Miller used his play to draw parallels between the Salem witch trials and the contemporary "witch hunts" led by Senator Joseph McCarthy against alleged communists. By depicting the hysteria and injustice faced by those accused, Miller critiqued the anti-communist sentiment gripping America. This connection helps readers see how political climates can influence the themes and messages within a dramatic work.

In addition to reflecting government actions, dramas capture significant societal changes, such as civil rights movements. Lorraine Hansberry's 'A Raisin in the Sun' is a powerful example of drama representing social change. The play depicts an African American family's struggle against racial segregation and economic hardship in Chicago. Through its characters and their experiences, Hansberry highlights the broader fight for civil rights and equality. Her portrayal of conflicting dreams and aspirations within the family mirrors the societal tensions of the time. Such representations showcase how playwrights use drama to advocate for and bring attention to necessary societal changes.

While dramas can be tools for social critique and advocacy, they are also subject to censorship. The impact of censorship on creative expression has historically shaped the content and themes of dramatic works. For instance, during the Elizabethan era, the authorities carefully scrutinised plays. William Shakespeare's 'Hamlet' includes subtle political commentary that had to navigate these restrictions. Words and scenes could be modified or omitted to avoid offending the monarchy or breaching social norms. Understanding how censorship influenced the narrative choices of playwrights like Shakespeare helps readers appreciate the authenticity and subversiveness embedded in classic works.

Cultural clashes and the concept of identity form another crucial aspect of drama, often portraying themes of belonging and community struggles. Consider August Wilson's 'Fences', which explores African American identity in the mid-20th century. The play's protagonist, Troy Maxson, battles with his past and the systemic racism that influenced his life decisions. Through his conflicts with his son and wife, Wilson delves into the broader cultural and generational divides within African American communities. This complexity enriches the narrative, showing how assimilating personal and communal identities can lead to conflict and understanding.

Guideline: When analysing dramas that reflect or critique government actions and policies, consider the historical context of when and why the play was written. Look for direct or indirect references to contemporary events within the dialogue and plot, assessing how these elements support or challenge existing power structures.

Moreover, dramas representing significant societal changes often feature characters who epitomise the struggle for justice and equality. Examining these characters' motivations and conflicts can provide deeper insights into the broader movements they symbolise. Plays like Hansberry's 'A Raisin in the Sun' offer valuable perspectives on how societal issues are woven into personal narratives, urging readers to look beyond individual struggles to understand collective challenges and aspirations.

Guideline: To effectively explore how playwrights advocate for societal change through drama, identify key characters and their roles within the depicted movement. Analyse their journeys and transformations to grasp the playwright's message about societal progress or stagnation.

Censorship's impact on drama isn't just historical; it continues to affect modern works. Contemporary playwrights may face similar constraints depending on their geographical and political landscapes. These restrictions can alter how sensitive topics are presented, prompting writers to find innovative ways to communicate their messages subtly. Recognising these constraints allows readers to critique the portrayed narrative's authenticity and the external pressures shaping it.

Guideline: When exploring the role of censorship in drama, investigate historical and modern examples to see how restrictions have influenced creative expressions. Compare censored versions with uncensored ones to understand the full scope of the intended message.

Finally, examining cultural clashes in dramas requires understanding the diverse influences shaping identity. Works like Wilson's 'Fences' highlight the intersections between cultural heritage and contemporary identity struggles. These dramas often use setting, language, and conflict to depict the richness and complexity of artistic experiences. Investigating these elements can reveal how playwrights address assimilation, resistance, and acceptance issues within a multicultural society.

Guideline: In analysing cultural conflicts within drama, focus on the interplay between characters' backgrounds and the socio-political environment they navigate. Pay attention to dialogue and symbolism that reflect cultural tensions and resolutions, enriching your understanding of the multifaceted nature of identity within dramatic works.

Economic Conditions and Patronage

Economic factors and influential patrons have long played a significant role in shaping the production and themes of drama. Understanding this relationship between art and economics can provide us with deeper insights into the motivations behind specific dramatic works and the conditions under which they were produced.

One key aspect to consider is how economic resources directly influence which stories are told in drama. A compelling example of this is seen during Shakespeare's era. Shakespeare lived in a time when the theatre was heavily reliant on the patronage of wealthy individuals and royalty. These patrons provided the financial support necessary for theatrical companies to produce plays, which often meant that the content of these plays had to appeal to the tastes and interests of their benefactors. For instance, many of Shakespeare's plays contained flattering references to his patrons or reflected the political climates they supported, showcasing how the presence of financial backing could shape narrative choices. This dependency on patronage ensured that themes and stories aligned closely with the desires of those funding the productions, thus affecting the creative freedom of playwrights.

Economic downturns also have a pronounced impact on the narratives presented in dramatic works. In times of economic crisis, themes of struggle and survival become more prominent as playwrights reflect societal conditions within their stories. For example, Arthur Miller's "Death of a Salesman" highlights the dire consequences of the American Dream amidst economic instability. The protagonist's downfall mirrors the financial despair felt by many during the post-World War II economic transitions in the United States. Similarly, during periods like the Great Depression, dramatic works often depicted the stark realities faced by everyday people, emphasising themes of poverty, loss, and resilience. By connecting the economic landscape with the characters' experiences, playwrights create a mirror through which audiences can see their struggles reflected in them.

Social class is another critical factor that shapes narrative and character interactions in drama. Class disparity is a common theme explored both in classic and contemporary literature. Take, for instance, the works of Henrik Ibsen, whose plays frequently examined the rigid class structures of 19th-century Norway. In "A Doll's House," Ibsen delves into the societal expectations placed upon the middle class, revealing how economic pressures influence personal relationships and individual identity. Similarly, Charles Dickens's "Great Expectations" portrays the profound impact of social class on its characters' aspirations and moral dilemmas, illustrating how class-based struggles can drive dramatic tension and enrich the storytelling. By focusing on class differences, dramatists highlight the inherent inequities within societies and prompt audiences to reflect on their societal constructs.

Moreover, commercialising drama across different eras reveals the delicate balance between maintaining artistic integrity and achieving commercial success. Theatre has always been subject to the economic realities of its time. During the 19th and early 20th centuries, the advent of the commercial theatre industry brought about significant changes in how dramas were produced and consumed. Playwrights and producers began to prioritise audience preferences and profitability, sometimes leading to artistic vision compromises. For example, George Bernard Shaw, known for his socially critical plays, often faced challenges gaining widespread acceptance due to the theatre industry's commercially driven nature. As a result, he had to balance his desire to address serious societal issues with the need to entertain and attract audiences. The trend continues today, with modern playwrights navigating commercial viability demands while striving to preserve the core messages within their works.

Guidelines for understanding the influence of economic factors on drama can be helpful for students, educators, and enthusiasts alike. Consider the following points:

Sources for Theater: Examine how financial resources from patrons, sponsors, or ticket sales influence dramas' content and production quality. Reflect on historical examples where patronage shaped creative output, such as during the Elizabethan era.

Fluctuations and Themes: Assess how economic conditions are mirrored in dramatic narratives. Identify plays that emerged during financial instability and analyse how these situations impacted the portrayal of characters and plotlines.

Structure and Drama: Explore how social class disparities are woven into the fabric of dramatic storytelling. Look at classic and modern works focusing on class struggles and consider how these narratives speak to broader societal issues.

as a Commercial Enterprise: Investigate the tension between artistic goals and commercial needs. Understand the historical context of theatre commercialisation and evaluate how playwrights balance the two forces in creating compelling yet marketable drama.

Cultural and Artistic Movements

Understanding the influence of cultural and artistic movements on drama is crucial for analysing historical context. Providing a contextual framework, we can better understand how various eras shaped dramatic works.

Romanticism and Realism are two significant movements that profoundly impacted characterisation and themes in drama. Romanticism, which flourished in the late 18th and early 19th centuries, emphasised emotion, individualism, and the sublime beauty of nature. Dramas from this period often feature highly emotional narratives, heroic characters, and a deep connection to nature and the human spirit. For instance, Goethe's "Faust" embodies the Romantic ideal of a protagonist driven by an insatiable quest for knowledge and experience, reflecting the movement's focus on intense personal emotions and the pursuit of the infinite.

In contrast, Realism emerged in the mid-19th century as a reaction against the perceived excesses of Romanticism. Focusing on everyday life and ordinary people, Realist dramatists sought to depict life accurately without romanticising it. This approach is evident in playwrights like Henrik Ibsen and Anton Chekhov, who portrayed complex characters facing real-life issues such as social inequality, marital strife, and existential crises. Ibsen's "A Doll's House" offers a stark portrayal of a woman challenging societal expectations, showcasing Realism's emphasis on truthful representations of individuals and their environments.

Moving into the 20th century, Modernism represented a radical departure from traditional narrative forms.

Modernist dramatists experimented with new storytelling techniques and structures, reflecting contemporary life's fragmented and chaotic nature. They often employed unconventional chronology, stream-of-consciousness writing, and abstract symbolism. For example, Samuel Beckett's "Waiting for Godot" eschews a linear plot in favour of repetitive dialogue and ambiguity, highlighting the futility and absurdity of human existence. This break from tradition allowed playwrights to explore deeper psychological and philosophical questions, thus broadening the scope of dramatic expression.

Postmodernism, emerging in the latter half of the 20th century, further challenged conventional narratives by rejecting the idea of objective meaning. Postmodern dramas frequently play with pastiche, irony, and self-referentiality, questioning the nature of reality and truth. Playwrights like Tom Stoppard exemplify this movement; his play "Rosencrantz and Guildenstern Are Dead" reinterprets Shakespeare's "Hamlet" through the eyes of two minor characters, blending humour and existential angst while undermining the notion of a singular, authoritative narrative. This approach engages audiences in a dialogue about multiple meanings and perspectives.

The influence of different cultures on local drama traditions and their contributions to global exchanges cannot be understated. Each culture brings unique elements to its dramatic works, informed by history, values, and social norms. For example, Japanese Noh theatre blends dance, music, and drama to create a highly stylised performance that differs significantly from Western traditions. The exchange of such diverse theatrical forms enriches global understanding and appreciation of universal themes like love, honour, and conflict.

Intercultural productions or adaptations allow for a fusion of styles and perspectives, enhancing the richness and diversity of the dramatic arts worldwide.

Revival movements also highlight the ongoing relevance of historical styles, drawing connections between past and present. These movements reflect a renewed interest in exploring and reinterpreting classical works within contemporary contexts. For instance, the resurgence of Shakespearean plays in modern times demonstrates how these timeless stories resonate with current audiences. Productions often update settings or themes to address contemporary societal issues, making the plays more accessible and relevant. The Globe Theatre's reconstruction and active performances illustrate this blend of historical authenticity and modern engagement, allowing audiences to connect with these works on multiple levels.

Understanding how these cultural and artistic movements shape drama provides valuable insights into the dynamic interplay between society and art. By studying Romanticism and Realism, we recognise the contrast between emotional narratives and realistic depictions of life. Modernism and Postmodernism challenge our perceptions of narrative and meaning, encouraging innovative expressions. The richness of various cultural traditions in drama underscores the global interconnectedness of artistic endeavours. Revival movements demonstrate classical styles' enduring power and relevance to contemporary audiences.

When analysing the historical context of dramatic works, one must consider these artistic movements' impact on style, themes, and reception. Recognising how each movement influenced playwrights and audiences helps us appreciate the complexities of interpreting drama across different eras. Whether it's the passionate intensity of Romanticism or the stark realism of 19th-century dramas, these influences provide a lens through which we can better understand the evolution of theatrical expression.

Moreover, acknowledging the global influences on drama highlights the importance of cross-cultural exchanges in enriching the art form. As we explore the myriad ways different societies contribute to the collective dramatic tradition, we gain a broader perspective on the universality of human experiences portrayed on stage. This understanding fosters a deeper appreciation for the diverse narratives that shape our cultural heritage and how they continue to inspire and challenge audiences today.

Impact on Interpretation and Reception

Understanding the historical context in which a drama was created is crucial for interpreting and appreciating its meaning. Historical context encompasses politics, society, economics, and culture, significantly influencing how audiences perceive a dramatic work. This subpoint will explore how historical context affects dramatic texts‘ interpretation and audience reception, fostering critical engagement with drama.

Firstly, the original context in which a play was produced profoundly impacted how its contemporary audience received it. For instance, plays like Shakespeare's "Hamlet" were shaped by the political and social environment of Elizabethan England. Local customs, beliefs, and the collective consciousness of the time influenced audience reactions in that period. Comparing these historical reactions to contemporary interpretations reveals shifts in societal values and attitudes. In modern times, “Hamlet” might be seen through various lenses, such as feminist, psychoanalytic, or post-colonial perspectives, reflecting current societal concerns. This comparison helps us understand the fluid nature of audience reception and the importance of situating a work within its original context.

Similarly, the perspective of critics is deeply rooted in their historical settings. Over different eras, critical approaches to dramatic works have evolved, reflecting broader intellectual and cultural trends. During the neoclassical period, criticism focused on adherence to classical unities and moral instruction. However, critics of the Romantic era valued emotional depth and individual expression. Today, postmodern critics often emphasise deconstruction and intertextuality. By understanding the changing landscape of critical reception, we can appreciate the multiplicity of interpretations a single dramatic text can inspire over time. These shifts underscore the importance of examining how historical context shapes critical viewpoints, enabling a richer engagement with the drama.

Intertextual references within plays also highlight the significance of historical context. Allusions to earlier texts, events, or cultural practices enrich many dramatic works. For example, T.S. Eliot’s play “Murder in the Cathedral” draws heavily on historical events and religious texts, creating layers of meaning that resonate differently across periods. Recognising these references allows audiences to uncover deeper messages and themes in the play. By situating these intertextual elements within their historical context, audiences and critics gain a more nuanced understanding of the work’s intentions and subsequent interpretations.

Modern adaptations of historical dramas play a critical role in maintaining the relevance of classic works. These adaptations often reinterpret the original plays to reflect contemporary issues and sensibilities. For example, Baz Luhrmann's 1996 film adaptation of "Romeo + Juliet" sets Shakespeare's timeless tragedy in modern-day Verona Beach, complete with contemporary costumes and settings. This new context allows today's audiences to connect with the story immediately and relevantly. Such reinterpretations reveal new meanings and demonstrate the enduring power of these works to speak to successive generations. The iterative engagement with historical dramas underscores how modern contexts can shed fresh light on age-old narratives.

To foster critical engagement with drama, it is essential to guide students, educators, and theatre enthusiasts in considering the historical context of the works they study. One effective guideline for young adult readers is to research the historical background of a play before delving into its analysis. Understanding the period in which it was written, the prevailing political and social conditions and the playwright's own experiences can provide invaluable insights into the play's themes and characters. For example, knowing that Arthur Miller wrote "The Crucible" during the Red Scare in the United States enriches our appreciation of its commentary on hysteria and persecution.

For educators and teachers, encouraging students to compare historical and contemporary receptions of dramatic works can deepen their analytical skills. Assigning readings of early reviews and more recent critiques can illustrate how interpretations evolve. Discussions in the classroom about why certain themes may have resonated more strongly with past audiences than with today's viewers can help students develop a sophisticated understanding of the relationship between a play and its context.

Theatre enthusiasts and amateur performers can benefit from exploring how intertextual references within a play contribute to its meaning. Engaging with source materials and historical texts referenced in a drama can uncover layers of significance that enhance their performance and interpretation. For example, actors performing in an "Oedipus Rex" production might consider the play's references to Greek mythology and ancient rituals to bring authenticity and depth to their portrayal of characters.

Furthermore, modern adaptations offer valuable opportunities for re-contextualizing historical dramas. Encouraging audiences to watch various adaptations and analyse how different directors interpret the exact text can reveal the versatility and adaptability of classic works. Performance workshops can include exercises where participants create adaptations, setting historical plays in new contexts to explore how these changes influence character motivations and plot development.

Role of Censorship

Censorship has long been a powerful force shaping the world of drama, affecting the creation and expression of theatrical works. Understanding its impact is crucial for appreciating how dramatic narratives evolve and respond to external pressures throughout history. Censorship influences the content and themes that playwrights explore and alters the portrayal of character experiences within their works.

Historically, censorship in drama has left a lasting imprint on the narratives we encounter. Governments, religious institutions, and societal norms have all imposed constraints on what could be depicted on stage. For instance, during the Elizabethan era, the Master of the Revels had the authority to approve or disapprove plays before they were performed. This control over dramatic content meant playwrights like William Shakespeare had to navigate strict guidelines to ensure their works saw the light of day. Consequently, certain themes, such as political dissent or explicit sexuality, were often toned down or masked through allegory and metaphor.

In the 20th century, various political regimes worldwide intensified censorship efforts, particularly under totalitarian states. In the Soviet Union, Socialist Realism became the mandated artistic style, requiring artists to highlight the virtues of communism and the Communist Party. Playwrights who deviated from this standard faced severe repercussions, including imprisonment or exile. This era demonstrated how censorship can suppress creative freedom, forcing dramatists to conform to state-sanctioned narratives and stifling innovation in dramatic form and content.

Understanding censorship helps critique the authenticity of depicted narratives by bridging historical examples with modern implications. When examining a play from a censored period, one must consider what the playwright attempted to convey within the limitations imposed upon them. This layer of analysis reveals hidden meanings and subtexts, providing richer interpretations of the text. Take, for example, Arthur Miller's "The Crucible," written during the McCarthy era in the United States. Though ostensibly about the Salem witch trials, the play serves as an allegory for the anti-communist hysteria of the time. Recognising the contextual censorship enhances our appreciation of Miller's commentary on paranoia and social persecution.

Examining different eras of censorship reveals how societal norms attempt to control artistic expression, impacting the diversity of narratives. In the Victorian era, strict moral codes dictated what was acceptable in literature and theatre. Plays addressing controversial topics such as women's rights, homosexuality, or critiques of the upper class were often banned or heavily edited. This suppression limited the scope of stories being told, resulting in a body of work that predominantly reflected the dominant culture's values.

Conversely, periods of relatively lax censorship can lead to a flourishing of diverse voices and innovative storytelling. The 1960s and 1970s in Western countries saw a relaxation of censorship laws, contributing to the rise of avant-garde theatre and experimental forms. Playwrights like Samuel Beckett and Harold Pinter broke conventional narrative structures, exploring existential themes and fragmented storytelling. This period underscored the importance of creative freedom in expanding the boundaries of dramatic expression and allowed marginalised perspectives to enter mainstream discourse.

Awareness of censorship practices enhances critical appraisal of the limitations imposed on dramatic works and their significance. By acknowledging the constraints under which playwrights operated, we gain a deeper understanding of their resilience and creativity. It highlights how artists adapt and resist through subtlety and subtext, pushing the envelope within the confines of acceptability.

Moreover, awareness of past censorship informs contemporary debates on free speech and artistic expression. Even today, censorship remains a contentious issue, with governments and institutions continuing to exert control over cultural productions. Recent examples include banning plays critical of political leaders or dealing with sensitive issues such as LGBTQ+ rights in various parts of the world. These modern instances echo historical patterns, reminding us of the struggle between artistic freedom and authoritative control.

Incorporating these insights into the drama study fosters a more nuanced appreciation of the art form. Educators can use examples of censorship to teach students about the historical context of plays, encouraging critical thinking about the forces that shape creative output. For young adults studying literature or drama, understanding censorship provides tools to analyse texts more deeply and recognise the interplay between societal pressures and artistic choices.

This knowledge equips educators and teachers to guide students toward a comprehensive analysis of dramatic works. Discussing censorship not only enhances literary criticism skills but also encourages discussions on broader themes such as freedom of expression, human rights, and the power dynamics between authority and the individual.

Theatre enthusiasts and amateur performers also benefit from understanding censorship's impact. Recognising playwrights' historical limitations can bring greater authenticity and depth to their performances. This awareness aids in portraying characters with the complexity intended by their creators, even when those intentions were cloaked in layers of compliance with censorship norms.

Summary and Reflections

Understanding the historical context in which a drama was created is essential for interpreting its meaning. Throughout this chapter, we have explored how political climates, social movements, economic conditions, and cultural influences shape dramatic narratives and the reception of these works. By analysing the historical background of plays, from the political critiques in Arthur Miller's "The Crucible" to societal reflections in Lorraine Hansberry's "A Raisin in the Sun," readers gain insight into the complex interplay between art and its environment. Recognising the impact of censorship and economic factors further enriches our appreciation of these narratives, revealing how external pressures can modify creative expression.

By examining diverse examples and their respective contexts, this chapter highlights the importance of situating dramas within their historical moments to grasp their deeper messages and significance. Whether confronting issues of identity in August Wilson's "Fences" or navigating the constraints of Shakespeare due to Elizabethan censorship, understanding these elements allows us to engage with dramatic texts on multiple levels critically. This awareness enhances our interpretation and fosters a greater connection to the timeless themes and struggles portrayed on stage, underscoring the relevance of historical context in the study of drama.

CHAPTER XI

Dramatic Techniques and Conventions

> *"Dramatic techniques and conventions are crucial in shaping how stories are told and experienced in a theatre. Playwrights employ these methods to craft compelling narratives, capture the audience's attention, and create immersive experiences that resonate deeply with viewers. By mastering various dramatic techniques, such as breaking the fourth wall, using dramatic irony, integrating flashbacks, and implementing non-linear narratives, playwrights can enhance their audiences' emotional and intellectual engagement, making each performance a memorable exploration of the human experience."*

This chapter delves into several key dramatic techniques and conventions used in theatre. It begins with exploring breaking the fourth wall, examining how this technique bridges the gap between actors and the audience to foster a sense of immediacy and involvement. Following this, the chapter discusses the use of dramatic irony to build suspense and emotional investment, highlighting its impact on character development and audience perception. The chapter then addresses the employment of flashbacks to provide crucial background information without disrupting the narrative flow. Additionally, it considers the application of non-linear narratives to challenge conventional storytelling and offer fresh perspectives on themes and characters. By understanding these techniques, readers will gain insights into how various elements contribute to the overall effectiveness of drama, ultimately enriching their appreciation and analysis of theatrical works.

Breaking the Fourth Wall

Breaking the fourth wall is a dramatic technique that allows characters to engage directly with the audience, creating a unique theatrical experience. This technique originates from theatre history and has fostered a sense of immediacy between the performance and the audience. It breaks the conventional barrier between the actors on stage and the spectators, making the audience an active participant in the narrative rather than a passive observer.

The phrase "breaking the fourth wall" comes from the traditional three-walled construct of a theatre stage: the two side walls, the back wall, and an imaginary fourth wall at the front of the stage through which the audience watches the play. By breaking this unseen boundary, characters can speak directly to the audience, share their thoughts, or comment on the action, bringing a new dimension to the storytelling process.

One prominent example of this technique can be found in Thornton Wilder's play "Our Town." In this play, the Stage Manager character frequently addresses the audience directly, providing context, offering commentary, and even inviting the audience to reflect on the presented themes. This direct engagement enhances the emotional connection between the characters and the viewers, fostering a deeper understanding and involvement in the story. The play transcends its traditional boundaries by involving the audience in this manner, creating an intimate and immediate shared experience.

Breaking the fourth wall also transforms passive observers into active participants. When characters acknowledge the audience's presence, it blurs the line between the play's fictional world and the audience's natural world. This interaction can provoke critical thought about the themes being explored within the drama. For instance, when characters address the audience and acknowledge social issues or moral dilemmas, they encourage viewers to reflect on these issues in their lives. The technique can be a powerful tool for raising awareness and prompting discussions long after the play ends.

However, breaking the fourth wall is not without its challenges. Poor execution can lead to confusion or alienation of the audience, causing a disconnect rather than engagement. Timing and context are crucial when employing this technique. If characters break the fourth wall without a clear purpose or relevance to the narrative, it can disrupt the flow of the story and diminish its impact. Therefore, careful consideration must be given to when and how this technique is used, ensuring it enhances rather than detracts from the overall performance.

In addition to timing and context, how characters address the audience is also significant. Direct engagement should feel natural and integral to the plot rather than forced or gimmicky. Successful examples of breaking the fourth wall blend seamlessly with the narrative, adding layers of meaning and depth to the story. Conversely, if the interaction feels jarring or out of place, it can break the suspension of disbelief and pull viewers out of the immersive experience.

Another important aspect to consider is the frequency of breaking the fourth wall. Overdoing it can lose its effectiveness and novelty, making it less impactful. A balanced approach ensures that the technique retains its ability to surprise and engage the audience. This balance can be achieved sparingly and strategically, allowing each occurrence to carry weight and significance.

Furthermore, the technique's effectiveness can vary depending on the genre and style of the play. In comedies, breaking the fourth wall often adds humour and a playful tone, while in dramas, it can introduce a level of seriousness and introspection. Understanding the nuances of the genre and the audience's expectations can guide the appropriate application of this technique, tailoring it to enhance the particular storytelling goals of the play.

Lastly, it's essential to recognise that breaking the fourth wall requires the actor's skill and charisma to engage the audience successfully. Actors must establish a rapport with the viewers and convey authenticity in their direct addresses. Their performance must bridge the gap between fiction and reality, inviting the audience to join them in the narrative journey.

Use of Dramatic Irony

Dramatic irony is an influential tool playwrights use to create suspense and depth in their storytelling. By definition, dramatic irony occurs when the audience knows about situations or events that the characters within the play do not. This disparity in knowledge heightens the audience's emotional investment, as they are acutely aware of the impending conflicts and consequences awaiting the characters.

One classic example of dramatic irony can be found in Shakespeare's 'Romeo and Juliet.' Here, the audience is privy to the fact that Juliet is not truly dead but has taken a potion to appear so. However, Romeo is unaware of this vital piece of information. The intense feelings of dread and anticipation this creates significantly magnify the stakes and complexity of the narrative. As Romeo approaches Juliet's seemingly lifeless body, audiences brace themselves for his tragic reaction, creating an emotionally charged atmosphere that underscores the play's themes of fate and miscommunication.

Moreover, dramatic irony compels audiences to anticipate moments of revelation eagerly. Knowing more than the characters allows the audience to predict potential outcomes and brace themselves for dramatic turns. This engagement encourages viewers to be more attentive and connected to the storyline, deepening their emotional experience. The tension built through dramatic irony keeps the viewers on the edge of their seats as they await the inevitable unravelling of the truth.

For instance, in 'Oedipus Rex' by Sophocles, dramatic irony is employed masterfully. The audience knows from the start that Oedipus himself is the cause of the plague afflicting Thebes, having killed his father and married his mother. However, he remains oblivious until the pivotal moment of realisation. This knowledge transforms every scene, conversation, and decision by Oedipus into a source of dramatic tension, as the audience foresees the tragic end long before the protagonist does. Such ironies compel the audience to engage deeply with the unfolding drama, experiencing the frustration and pathos of Oedipus's journey.

Characters often appear foolish or tragically misguided based on their ignorance of crucial facts, enriching the audience's analysis of their motivations and actions. This feature of dramatic irony invites critical thinking, prompting viewers to delve deeper into the reasons behind the characters' decisions and behaviours. It also accentuates human vulnerability and folly, making the characters' arcs more relatable and poignant. In essence, characters become more richly developed and their stories more compelling due to the layers of meaning added by dramatic irony.

Take, for example, the character of Malvolio in Shakespeare's 'Twelfth Night.' His self-deception and mistaken belief in Olivia's love for him, spurred by a forged letter, lead to comedic yet pitiable situations. The audience's awareness of the trick being played on Malvolio creates a blend of humour and sympathy, as his ignorance amplifies his character's comic and tragic elements. This duality enriches the play and offers a nuanced look at themes of pride, ambition, and social status.

The superior knowledge granted to the audience through dramatic irony also cultivates a unique bond between the audience and the overall narrative. This shared understanding makes the audience feel more involved in the story, almost like they are participants rather than mere observers. This bond is particularly evident in thriller and horror genres, where dramatic irony is utilised to build nail-biting suspense. By letting the audience in on secrets unknown to the characters, playwrights can precisely manipulate their emotions and reactions, guiding them through a rollercoaster of anticipation, dread, and relief.

Consider Arthur Miller's 'The Crucible,' where the audience is aware of Abigail Williams' deceit and manipulation throughout the witch trials, while many characters are not. This use of dramatic irony intensifies the sense of desperation and injustice as innocent people are accused and punished. The audience's frustration mirrors the chaos and hysteria within the Salem community, helping them grasp the broader implications of mass paranoia and integrity under duress.

Flashbacks and Foreshadowing

Flashbacks and foreshadowing are key techniques that playwrights use to enhance the narrative structure and thematic depth of their works. By understanding how these elements function, readers can appreciate the intricate construction of drama and its impact on audiences.

Flashbacks are powerful for providing context to characters' backgrounds and motivations. Their use allows playwrights to delve into the past without disrupting the present storyline. This technique is effectively demonstrated in Arthur Miller's "Death of a Salesman." In the play, the protagonist, Willy Loman, frequently experiences flashbacks that reveal crucial aspects of his life, such as his relationship with his brother Ben and his disappointment in his son Biff. These scenes provide a deeper understanding of Willy's current struggles and aspirations, making his character more complex and relatable. The inclusion of flashbacks allows the audience to see the continuity between the past and present, reinforcing themes of memory, regret, and the unattainable American Dream.

On the other hand, foreshadowing is employed to build suspense and anticipation by hinting at future developments. William Shakespeare's "Macbeth" offers a masterful example of foreshadowing through the prophecy of the three witches. When the witches predict Macbeth's rise to power and eventual downfall, they set the stage for the unfolding drama. This early indication creates an atmosphere of tension and inevitability that permeates the entire play. Each subsequent event and choice Macbeth makes is tinged with the foreboding knowledge of his destined fate. This technique keeps the audience engaged as they watch the character's actions with heightened awareness and emotional investment.

The combined use of flashbacks and foreshadowing can create layered narratives that deepen dramatic tension. Playwrights can construct a rich tapestry of interconnected moments by interweaving past events with hints of what is to come. For instance, in Tennessee Williams' "The Glass Menagerie," flashbacks contribute to the play's non-linear structure, allowing the audience to piece together the fragmented lives of the Wingfield family. Meanwhile, subtle foreshadowing hints at the impending disintegration of their dreams and aspirations. This interplay enriches the narrative and adds emotional resonance as viewers experience the total weight of past decisions on future outcomes.

However, the timing of flashbacks and foreshadowing is critical to their effectiveness. Poorly timed flashbacks can disrupt the narrative flow and confuse the audience. Similarly, heavy-handed or misplaced foreshadowing can diminish suspense rather than enhance it. Successful examples of these techniques demonstrate a balance that maintains narrative coherence and emotional engagement. For instance, in "Death of a Salesman," the flashbacks are seamlessly integrated into the present-day scenes, often triggered by specific stimuli or emotional states. This careful placement ensures the audience remains oriented while gaining essential insights into Willy's character.

Likewise, in Macbeth, foreshadowing is woven into the dialogue and action in a way that feels organic rather than contrived. The witches' prophecies appear almost incidental yet carry significant weight throughout the play. This subtlety allows the foreshadowing to build tension naturally as the plot advances rather than overwhelming the narrative with constant reminders of future events. Such balanced execution exemplifies how these techniques can enhance storytelling without overshadowing it.

Non-linear Narratives

Non-linear narratives disrupt traditional storytelling by presenting events out of their natural chronological order. This technique creates unique dramatic experiences that can deeply engage audiences and offer fresh perspectives on characters and themes. By breaking away from a linear sequence, playwrights can emphasise themes of memory and perception, illustrating how these elements shape human experience and understanding.

One notable example of the non-linear narrative is Tennessee Williams' play "The Glass Menagerie." In this play, the story unfolds in a series of memories narrated by the protagonist, Tom Wingfield. The unconventional structure reflects the fragmented and subjective nature of memory. Williams delves into the characters' psychological states through this approach and highlights how past events influence their present lives. By juxtaposing different time frames, the audience gains insight into each character's motivations and inner conflicts, particularly Tom, his sister Laura, and their mother Amanda. This method enhances the emotional complexity of the narrative, making it more relatable and poignant.

Non-linear narratives also challenge audience expectations, prompting viewers to engage more actively with the story. Traditional linear storytelling often leads the audience along a predictable path, with events unfolding cause and effect. In contrast, non-linear narratives require audiences to piece together the plot, encouraging them to think critically about the connections between scenes. This active engagement fosters a deeper understanding of character motivations and the thematic underpinnings of the play. As audiences strive to make sense of the disordered timeline, they become more invested in the narrative and the characters' journeys.

However, non-linear narratives come with potential pitfalls. If not executed carefully, they can confuse the audience, obscuring the storyline and diminishing its impact. The key to successful implementation is maintaining clear connections between events, even when presented out of order. Using motifs, recurring symbols, or thematic links can help guide the audience through the narrative maze. When done well, these techniques ensure that the story remains coherent and impactful despite the non-linear structure.

The emphasis on memory and perception through non-linear storytelling allows playwrights to explore complex themes innovatively. Memory is inherently subjective and selective, often coloured by emotions and personal biases. By structuring a play around fragmented recollections, writers can portray how characters reinterpret and reshape their pasts. This approach enriches character development and invites the audience to reflect on their perceptions and memories. It highlights the idea that no singular truth exists but multiple, intertwined perspectives that contribute to one's understanding of reality.

In addition to "The Glass Menagerie," other contemporary works effectively utilise non-linear narratives to similar effect. For instance, Harold Pinter's play "Betrayal" employs a reverse chronological order, starting with the end of an affair and moving backwards to its beginning. This structure reveals the gradual disintegration of relationships and trust, offering a profound commentary on human interactions and deceit. Seeing the consequences before the causes gives the audience a unique perspective on the characters' actions and the inevitability of certain outcomes.

Another example is Michael Cunningham's novel "The Hours," which was later adapted into a film. The story weaves together three disparate timelines, linking the lives of Virginia Woolf, a 1950s housewife and a modern-day editor. Although the narratives are separated by decades, their thematic connections—such as struggles with identity and the pursuit of meaning—bind them together. This non-linear approach allows for a rich exploration of how different generations confront similar existential questions, underscoring the timeless nature of these themes.

While non-linear narratives can deepen thematic exploration and audience engagement, they also demand careful handling to avoid disorienting viewers. Playwrights and directors must strike a balance between artistic innovation and clarity. Providing enough context within each scene, using visual or auditory cues, and establishing solid thematic threads can help maintain coherence. Even a non-linear narrative can be navigated smoothly when these elements are in place, ensuring its intended emotional and intellectual impacts are fully realised.

The challenges of non-linear storytelling highlight the importance of thoughtful construction and deliberate choices. A well-crafted non-linear narrative can transform a simple story into a multi-layered, dynamic experience. Conversely, a poorly executed one risks alienating the audience and diluting the story's power. Therefore, it is crucial for writers and directors to thoroughly understand the implications of their structural decisions and consistently evaluate whether their approach serves the overall narrative and theme.

Challenges and Risks in Dramatic Techniques

Exploring the potential pitfalls and challenges in implementing various dramatic techniques offers significant insights for young adults studying literature, educators, and theatre enthusiasts alike. By examining these obstacles, readers can better understand how to approach and analyse different elements of drama effectively.

Breaking the fourth wall is a technique where characters speak directly to the audience, blurring the lines between fiction and reality. When well-executed, it can create an engaging and intimate experience. However, if poorly implemented, it risks confusing or alienating the audience. For instance, if the transition between addressing the audience and the narrative flow is abrupt or unmotivated, viewers may struggle to follow the story. The intent behind breaking the fourth wall must be clear and purposeful, ensuring that it enhances rather than detracts from the narrative.

Dramatic irony is another powerful tool in a playwright's arsenal, creating a disparity between what the audience knows and what the characters know. This technique heightens tension and emotional investment as the audience anticipates the unfolding events. However, overuse of dramatic irony can backfire by making characters seem unrealistically ignorant or foolish. In high school settings, students might recall Shakespeare's 'Romeo and Juliet,' where the audience is painfully aware of the tragic misunderstanding between the protagonists. While this works within the context of the play, excessive reliance on dramatic irony in other contexts can diminish its impact, rendering characters less relatable and believable.

Flashbacks provide background information, revealing crucial details about a character's past. When integrated seamlessly, they add depth and context, enriching the narrative. Conversely, inadequately timed flashbacks might bewilder audiences, disrupting the flow of the story. For example, if a flashback occurs without proper setup or foreshadowing, it can leave viewers questioning its relevance. A balanced approach, where flashbacks are strategically placed to enhance understanding rather than distract, is essential.

Non-linear narratives challenge conventional storytelling by presenting events out of chronological order. This technique can emphasise themes of memory and perception, offering unique dramatic experiences. However, non-linear narratives require careful construction and motivation to maintain coherence. Without clear connections between events, audiences can easily become lost or disengaged. A compelling non-linear narrative should guide the viewer through its complex structure, ensuring that each scene contributes meaningfully to the plot.

In educational settings, it's important to highlight these potential pitfalls and challenges when teaching dramatic techniques. Students should be encouraged to critically analyse how these methods are used in various plays and their effect on the audience. Understanding the risks associated with these techniques allows for more thoughtful and nuanced interpretations of dramatic works.

Additionally, aspiring playwrights and performers should consider these challenges when incorporating dramatic techniques. Practice and feedback are instrumental in refining their use of these methods. By experimenting with breaking the fourth wall, practitioners can discover how to balance engagement with clarity. Similarly, the judicious use of dramatic irony can evoke desired emotional responses without undermining character credibility.

Writers should develop a keen sense of timing for flashbacks, ensuring each one serves a specific purpose in advancing the story or deepening character development. Non-linear narratives demand meticulous planning, and each non-chronological segment must align with the play's thematic and emotional arc.

Theatre educators can support students by providing exercises that hone these skills. For instance, staging scenes with and without breaking the fourth wall can illustrate its effects on audience engagement. Analysing examples of dramatic irony in classic and contemporary works can help students appreciate its strengths and limitations. Workshops focusing on crafting coherent flashbacks and non-linear stories can foster a deeper understanding of these techniques.

What We Learnt

In this chapter, we have delved deeply into various dramatic techniques and conventions that playwrights use to enhance storytelling and engage the audience. By exploring methods such as breaking the fourth wall, dramatic irony, flashbacks, and non-linear narratives, readers can better understand how these elements create powerful and immersive theatrical experiences. These techniques add layers to the narrative and provoke thought and emotional responses from the audience, making the drama more engaging and impactful.

By understanding the importance of timing, context, and execution, readers can appreciate the intricate craft behind successful plays. Whether you are a student studying literature, an educator guiding young minds, or an enthusiast looking to deepen your appreciation for theatre, these insights provide valuable tools for analysing and interpreting dramatic works. Mastering these techniques requires practice and thoughtful consideration, leading to more prosperous and meaningful storytelling.

CHAPTER XII

Case Studies from World Literature

Examining plays through the lens of analytical techniques unveils the complex layers of structure, theme, and character in world literature. This chapter aims to equip readers with the tools to dissect these dramatic elements, using case studies from various notable works across history and contemporary literature. By focusing on well-known plays such as "Oedipus Rex," "Hamlet," "A Doll's House," and "Waiting for Godot," we can illustrate how analytical methods bring depth and clarity to our understanding of drama.

The chapter will begin with an analysis of ancient Greek tragedies, highlighting "Oedipus Rex" by Sophocles to explore the interplay between fate and character. Following this, the focus shifts to the complexities within Shakespearean drama, specifically examining themes and character development in "Hamlet." Henrik Ibsen's "A Doll's House " then represents modern drama," discussing gender roles and societal expectations. Finally, the chapter delves into postmodern drama with Samuel Beckett's "Waiting for Godot," emphasising existentialism and the absurd. Each section will analyse the structure and themes and provide contextual understanding to enrich readers' interpretations of these timeless works.

Greek Tragedies: Oedipus Rex

One of the most significant works of ancient Greek tragedy, Oedipus Rex, is a quintessential example of how structure and themes can illuminate various aspects of fate and character development. This subpoint delves into the structural design and thematic depth of Oedipus Rex to provide a detailed understanding.

Firstly, the structure of Oedipus Rex is critical in grasping its narrative power. The play follows a traditional but effective structure composed of four main parts: exposition, rising action, climax, and resolution. The exposition introduces us to King Oedipus of Thebes, a respected ruler who seeks to save his city from a devastating plague. As the story progresses into the rising action, Oedipus's determined quest to find the murderer of the previous king, Laius, sets the stage for his tragic downfall. Here, dramatic irony plays a crucial role, as the audience is already aware of Oedipus's fate, creating an engaging tension that heightens emotional investment.

Moving onto the climax, the intense revelation scene where Oedipus realises that he is the murderer of Laius and marries his mother, Jocasta, marks the peak of the play's dramatic tension. The final part, the resolution, sees Oedipus accepting his fate by blinding himself and going into exile, encapsulating the inevitability of fate—a central theme in Greek tragedies.

Analysing this structural elegance reveals that inevitable fate profoundly impacts characters' choices and relationships. Such analysis not only unpacks the mechanics of the plot but also provides insights into how ancient Greeks perceived destiny and human agency. Tragic fate in Oedipus Rex reflects the ancient belief that humans cannot escape their predetermined destinies, regardless of their actions. This view is further emphasised by using oracles and prophetic declarations throughout the play, underlining the omnipotent influence of fate over free will.

Another compelling theme within Oedipus Rex is blindness and insight. The play masterfully juxtaposes physical blindness with metaphorical blindness to explore concepts of knowledge and ignorance. Tiresias, the blind prophet, embodies true insight despite his lack of physical sight. In contrast, Oedipus, who possesses physical vision, remains metaphorically blind to the truth of his origins and actions. He gains profound insight into his life and fate only after he loses everything—his status, family, and literal sight. This inversion reinforces the tragedy of Oedipus's pride and ignorance and underscores the complexity of human perception and the painful journey toward self-awareness.

The dynamic between Oedipus and Tiresias illuminates a broader struggle between knowledge and denial. When Tiresias confronts Oedipus with the truth about his past, Oedipus vehemently rejects it, accusing Tiresias of conspiracy. This conflict showcases Oedipus's initial resistance to accepting his doomed fate and his role in fulfilling the prophecy. Similarly, Jocasta's role adds emotional depth to the narrative. She transitions from a reassuring presence to a tragic figure overwhelmed by the horrifying realisation of the truth. Her eventual suicide amplifies the emotional gravity and inevitability of the tragic events, making her more than just a secondary character but rather a pivotal figure whose actions and emotions deeply affect the dramatic arc.

Understanding the cultural and historical context in which Oedipus Rex was written enriches our interpretation of the play. Ancient Greek society placed immense value on fate and morality, believing that the gods controlled human destinies and that defying prophetic truths brought dire consequences. The moral lessons embedded in Greek tragedies were meant to resonate with the audience, reflecting on hubris, justice, and divine intervention. Examining these societal values gives one a greater appreciation for the characters' motivations and expectations. For example, despite the risks, Oedipus's determination to uncover the truth aligns with Greek ideals of heroism and resilience. His ultimate punishment is a cautionary tale against excessive pride and the dangers of seeking forbidden knowledge.

Shakespearean Plays: Hamlet

Analysing character complexity and thematic depth in "Hamlet" is essential to appreciating Shakespeare's drama, which remains relevant today. One of the most intricate aspects of the play is Hamlet's character. His multifaceted personality reflects a universal human experience marked by indecision, moral dilemmas, and a profound sense of doubt and action. Hamlet's internal struggle is palpable as he oscillates between the desire for revenge and a hesitation that stems from deep moral contemplation. This narrative mirrors individuals' real-life experiences when grappling with significant life decisions, making Hamlet a timeless character whose problems resonate across different eras.

Hamlet's famous soliloquies are vital to understanding his inner thoughts and motivations. These moments allow the audience direct access to his mind, showcasing his rationality, self-doubt, and philosophical musings. For instance, the iconic "To be or not to be" soliloquy delves into existential questions about life, death, and the purpose of existence. By verbalising these thoughts, Hamlet engages the audience deeper, prompting them to reflect on their beliefs and uncertainties. Soliloquies thus act as a bridge between Hamlet and the audience, facilitating empathy and understanding.

Madness and identity are central themes in "Hamlet." The protagonist's feigned madness serves multiple purposes within the narrative. It acts as a strategic cover to investigate his father's suspicious death and disarm potential threats while also raising questions about reality versus performance. Hamlet's apparent descent into madness blurs the line between genuine insanity and calculated behaviour, emphasising the theme of authenticity. This complexity invites readers to ponder the nature of sanity and the masks people wear in societal interactions.

The recurring motif of madness extends beyond Hamlet to other characters, such as Ophelia. Unlike Hamlet's, her madness appears genuine and is triggered by external pressures, including her father's death and Hamlet's rejection. Ophelia's trajectory contrasts sharply with Hamlet's controlled façade of insanity, offering another lens to view the destructive power of grief and loss. This juxtaposition further complicates the play's exploration of mental states and identities, enriching its thematic depth.

Understanding the political and social context of "Hamlet" is crucial for grasping the motivations behind the character's actions and plot unfolding. The tensions of royal power struggles are evident from the outset, with Claudius's usurpation of the throne creating an atmosphere of corruption and distrust. This backdrop of political intrigue informs Hamlet's quest for revenge, as his actions are driven not only by personal grievances but also by a larger sense of justice and the moral decay of the state.

The corrupt nature of the court under Claudius's rule casts a shadow over the entire narrative, influencing the behaviours and decisions of various characters. The political machinations depicted in the play reflect broader concerns about leadership, legitimacy, and the impact of power on human relationships. This aspect of the play continues to be relevant in contemporary discussions about governance and ethics, demonstrating the enduring significance of Shakespearean drama.

In studying Hamlet, it is essential to consider how the interplay of personal and political elements creates a rich tapestry of themes and character dynamics. Shakespeare masterfully weaves these threads, portraying a world where individual struggles are deeply intertwined with broader societal issues. This fusion ensures that "Hamlet" remains a compelling subject for analysis, offering insights into both the human condition and the complexities of social structures.

An effective way to approach this analysis is to focus on specific scenes highlighting these themes and character developments. For example, the play-within-a-play scene is a critical moment where Hamlet uses theatrical performance to expose Claudius's guilt. This meta-theatrical device underscores the theme of appearance versus reality and demonstrates Hamlet's cunning use of drama for truth-seeking. Examining such scenes can provide a more detailed understanding of how Shakespeare employs dramatic techniques to convey profound messages.

Additionally, exploring the historical and cultural context in which "Hamlet" was written can enrich one's interpretation of the text. Recognising the influences of Elizabethan attitudes towards monarchy, religion, and philosophy can offer valuable perspectives on the play's themes and character motivations. For instance, Hamlet's reflective nature and existential inquiries reflect the Renaissance's emphasis on humanism and individualism. Understanding these cultural underpinnings can deepen our appreciation of the play's complexity and resonance with past and present audiences.

Modern Plays: A Doll's House

Henrik Ibsen's "A Doll's House" is pivotal in that it explores gender roles and societal expectations. Through its well-crafted narrative and complex characters, the play sheds light on the dynamics of marriage, individuality, and the façade of domestic bliss. This subpoint explores these themes and their relevance in contemporary discourse.

One of the most compelling elements of "A Doll's House" is the characterisation of Nora, the protagonist. Nora's journey of self-discovery is central to understanding the impact of societal constraints on individual identity. Throughout the play, Nora evolves from a seemingly naive, subservient wife to an assertive woman who recognises her worth beyond societal expectations. Initially, she appears to conform to the traditional roles expected of her—caring for her children, managing household duties, and adhering to her husband's wishes. However, as the plot unfolds, we witness Nora's growing awareness of the limitations placed upon her by society and her family. Her ultimate decision to leave her husband and children is a radical act of self-liberation, highlighting the oppressive nature of prescribed gender roles and the necessity for personal autonomy. This transformation underscores the notion that true identity can only be realised when one steps outside societal confines.

Closely tied to Nora's characterisation are the overarching themes of marriage and identity that permeate the play. The façade of a perfect household that Nora and her husband, Torvald, maintain reveals deeper issues about inequality and personal sacrifice within marital dynamics. On the surface, their marriage appears ideal, with Torvald assuming the role of a benevolent provider and Nora as the dutiful wife. However, this veneer masks underlying discontent and imbalance. Torvald's condescending treatment of Nora and his preoccupation with social appearances reflect patriarchal values that prioritise male authority and female subservience. Nora's eventual rebellion against this dynamic exposes the superficiality of their relationship and the broader societal expectations that perpetuate such inequalities. By presenting the tumultuous reality beneath the "perfect" marriage, Ibsen critiques the traditional institution of marriage and advocates for a more equitable partnership based on mutual respect and individual fulfilment.

The symbolism of the doll's house itself is another crucial aspect of the play, effectively encapsulating thematic messages about personal agency and appearance versus reality within domestic spaces. The title "A Doll's House" reflects Nora's life—a beautifully crafted exterior that hides a controlled existence. Just as a dollhouse is meticulously arranged and confined, so is Nora's life dictated by her husband's whims and societal norms. This motif also extends to the other characters, suggesting that societal expectations similarly constrain many lives. The doll's house becomes a powerful symbol of the lack of agency experienced by individuals, especially women, within rigid domestic frameworks. The contrast between the outwardly charming home and its restrictive internal dynamics illustrates the disparity between appearance and reality, urging audiences to question and challenge societal constructs that stifle personal growth.

The cultural impact of "A Doll's House" cannot be overstated, as its themes have sparked enduring societal debates regarding gender equality and personal rights. Upon its release in the late 19th century, the play elicited significant backlash for its controversial portrayal of a woman abandoning her familial duties in pursuit of self-identity. Critics and audiences alike were divided, with some condemning Nora's actions as morally reprehensible, while others lauded Ibsen's bold critique of societal norms. This polarised reception underscores the contentious nature of gender roles and the struggle for gender equality that continues to this day. By challenging the status quo and presenting a narrative that prioritises individual rights over societal expectations, "A Doll's House" has become a seminal text in feminist literature. It not only reflects historical attitudes towards gender but also provides valuable insight into ongoing discourses surrounding personal autonomy and gender-based oppression.

In contemporary discourse, "A Doll's House" remains highly relevant. Modern audiences can draw parallels between Nora's struggles and the persistent challenges individuals, particularly women, face in asserting their identities and rights within societal structures. The play encourages a critical examination of how far society has progressed in terms of gender equality and highlights areas where further change is needed. For young adults studying literature or drama, "A Doll's House" is a powerful example of how dramatic works can address and influence social issues. It provides educators with a rich text to explore themes of identity, agency, and societal expectations, fostering critical thinking and empathy among students. For theatre enthusiasts and performers, understanding the depth of these themes can enhance their appreciation of the play and inform more nuanced portrayals of its characters.

Postmodern Drama: Waiting for Godot

Samuel Beckett's "Waiting for Godot" is a significant work in modern theatre. It showcases themes of existentialism and absurdity. This play's unique structure, character dynamics, and thematic elements offer deep insights into human existence, making it a valuable subject for analysis.

Firstly, the absurdist elements inherent in the "Waiting for Godot" structure are essential to understand. The play follows a cyclical narrative that defies conventional plot structures. Unlike traditional dramas with clear beginnings, climaxes, and resolutions, Beckett's work loops back on itself. This lack of progression mirrors everyday life's repetitive and often seemingly meaningless routines, emphasising a core tenet of existentialism: the search for meaning in an indifferent universe. By presenting events that recur without resolution, Beckett disrupts audience expectations and forces them to confront the possibility that life may lack inherent direction or purpose.

The cyclical nature also highlights the characters' sense of waiting, which is central to the play's dramatic tension. Estragon and Vladimir wait for someone named Godot, who never arrives, encapsulating the endless nature of waiting itself. This unfulfilled anticipation reflects existential despair, illustrating how humans persistently seek purpose despite uncertainty. The absence of a conventional climax pushes viewers to question the significance of their pursuits and the perpetual hope for answers or resolutions that may never come. Beckett challenges the audience to reconsider their understanding of time and progress through this structure.

Vladimir and Estragon's relationship is another pivotal aspect that enriches the existential themes of "Waiting for Godot." Their interactions are marked by companionship and isolation, raising deep philosophical questions about human connections. Despite their constant bickering and contemplation of separation, they remain together, highlighting the dual nature of human relationships. On one hand, their reliance on each other signifies the basic human need for companionship; on the other, it underscores the loneliness inherent in individual existence since neither truly comprehends the other's inner world.

Their dialogues, filled with nonsensical and repetitive exchanges, reflect the absurdity of language as a tool for communication. Language, typically seen as a bridge between individuals, becomes a source of confusion and distraction rather than understanding. This dynamic suggests that while humans crave connection, proper comprehension remains elusive, emphasising existential solitude. Such portrayal of character dynamics prompts audiences to reflect on their interpersonal relationships and the balance between dependence on others and fundamental isolation.

Moving from character dynamics to broader themes, the time motif pervades "Waiting for Godot," compelling deeper analysis of human perception of time and existence. The act of waiting becomes a lens through which existential concerns are magnified. Time in the play appears fluid and ambiguous, contributing to the overall sense of uncertainty.

Days blend, and Estragon and Vladimir often struggle to recall past events, signifying a break from the linear, measured time typically experienced daily.

This manipulation of time aligns with existential thought by questioning its relevance and impact on human experience. Since time does not lead to any significant change or progression in the play, it posits that forward movement in life might be an illusion, and actual experiences might be more cyclic than linear. Despite its apparent futility, the characters' continuous waiting mirrors the human condition, where people often wait for events or realisations that could provide their lives with meaning, revealing an inherent absurdity in such expectations.

Moreover, Beckett's treatment of existential themes is not only relevant within the context of the play but also extends its influence to contemporary theatre. His postmodern techniques, such as breaking away from logical narrative structures and emphasising the irrational aspects of life, have paved the way for new forms of drama. These methods allow playwrights to tackle complex existential dilemmas innovatively, shifting focus from traditional storytelling to exploration of consciousness, identity, and reality.

Modern dramas influenced by Beckett often feature fragmented narratives, antiheroes, and metafictional elements—all tools to delve into the intricacies of human existence. For instance, playwrights like Harold Pinter and Tom Stoppard have adopted and expanded upon Beckettian motifs to further address topics of alienation, identity crisis, and the pursuit of meaning. The legacy of "Waiting for Godot" thus lies in its ability to inspire and reshape theatrical expression continuously, encouraging creators and audiences to engage deeply with the essence of what it means to exist.

General Analytical Techniques in Drama

Identifying Structural Elements: Understanding a play's structure is a crucial first step in analysing it. Discerning the narrative's framework, readers can better grasp how key events and turning points are interwoven to create a cohesive story. Traditional plays often follow a clear-cut structure comprising an exposition, rising action, climax, falling action, and resolution. This Aristotelian model is a blueprint that guides writers and analysts in mapping out the plot's trajectory.

For instance, in Shakespeare's *Romeo and Juliet*, the exposition introduces the feuding families and sets up the central conflict involving Romeo and Juliet's forbidden love. As we move into the rising action, their secret marriage escalates tensions, leading to the climax with Mercutio and Tybalt's deaths. The falling action captures the couple's attempts to reunite amidst escalating challenges, culminating in the tragic resolution where they both die. Understanding this structure allows us to pinpoint pivotal moments that change the course of the narrative, offering insights into character motivations and thematic evolutions.

Exploring Central Themes: Another vital analytical technique involves delving into the recurring themes within a play. Themes act as the backbone that supports the narrative, offering deeper meanings and reflections on societal issues or human experiences. By identifying and exploring central themes, readers can enhance their comprehension of the core messages that the playwright intends to convey.

Take Arthur Miller's *The Crucible* as an example. One prominent theme is the hysteria that grips the community during the Salem witch trials. Through the characters' actions and dialogues, Miller critiques the dangers of mass paranoia and the consequences of unfounded accusations. Further analysis of this theme reveals how fear can erode trust and moral integrity, leading individuals to commit heinous acts under the guise of righteousness. Such thematic exploration encourages readers to draw parallels between the play and contemporary societal issues, enriching their understanding of the text.

Character Analysis: In addition to structural and thematic analysis, examining character interactions and development is essential for uncovering more enormous thematic and narrative implications. Playwrights express ideas, conflicts, and emotional journeys through characters, making it imperative for readers to analyse their roles and transformations throughout the play.

Consider Tennessee Williams' *A Streetcar Named Desire.* Blanche DuBois and Stanley Kowalski represent contrasting worlds—Blanche's fragile, illusionary existence versus Stanley's raw, visceral reality. Blanche's descent into madness and Stanley's relentless dominance highlight the struggle between appearances and reality, revealing the play's broader commentary on human vulnerability and societal expectations. Analysing the nuanced dynamics between these characters provides deeper insights into the psychological and social undercurrents driving the narrative.

Contextual Understanding: Lastly, placing a dramatic work within its cultural, historical, and social context adds significant depth to its interpretation. Contextual understanding helps readers appreciate the influences and circumstances that shape the play's content, themes, and character portrayals.

For example, Lorraine Hansberry's *A Raisin in the Sun* is deeply rooted in the socio-political climate of 1950s America, particularly within the African American community facing systemic racism and economic hardships. The Younger family's struggles and aspirations reflect broader societal issues of racial discrimination, housing segregation, and the pursuit of the American Dream. By examining the cultural and historical context, readers can better understand the significance of the characters' experiences and the play's impact on the discourse surrounding civil rights and social justice.

What We Learnt

This chapter has examined the application of analytical techniques to various historical and contemporary plays. By analysing works such as "Oedipus Rex," "Hamlet," "A Doll's House," and "Waiting for Godot," we have delved into how structure, themes, and characters can be dissected to reveal deeper meanings. Studying these elements provides a richer understanding of each play and demonstrates how dramatic works reflect broader societal and philosophical issues. Furthermore, exploring structural aspects, central themes, character interactions, and contextual understanding has been highlighted as essential tools for effective analysis.

Through practical examples, readers can use strategies to engage more deeply with dramatic texts. This analysis emphasises the importance of recognising how playwrights use structural and thematic devices to convey complex ideas. In doing so, it fosters critical thinking and an appreciation for the multifaceted nature of drama. Whether for young students, educators, or theatre enthusiasts, mastering these analytical techniques enhances their ability to interpret and enjoy dramatic literature, thereby enriching their overall engagement with the art form.

Conclusion

> "*As we conclude our exploration into the world of drama, it's essential to revisit the key themes and concepts woven throughout this book. Each chapter has offered a unique perspective on the multifaceted nature of dramatic works, allowing us to delve into the philosophical underpinnings of Greek tragedies, the complex emotional landscapes portrayed in character-centric narratives, and the transformative power of performance. By reflecting on these intricate layers, it becomes evident that drama is far more than mere entertainment; it is a profound medium through which we can explore and understand the human experience.*"

In the initial chapters, we examined the origins of drama, tracing its roots back to ancient civilisations, where it served both as a form of ritual and social commentary. The timeless themes of fate, morality, and the human condition central to Greek tragedies continue to resonate with audiences today. These early explorations provided a foundation for understanding the enduring relevance of dramatic works, illustrating how they mirror societal values and challenges across different eras.

Moving forward, we delved into the rich tapestry of character development, emphasising the importance of emotional depth in creating compelling narratives. Through various case studies, we explored how playwrights craft believable characters that reflect diverse human experiences. This focus on characterisation enabled us to appreciate the nuances of personal conflict, growth, and transformation that drive the narrative forward. As readers and viewers, this more profound understanding of character motivations enhances our engagement with the story, making the experience more immersive and impactful.

Examining different dramatic genres further enriched our understanding of the art form. From melodrama's heightened emotions and moral dilemmas of melodrama to the satirical wit of comedies, each genre offers unique opportunities for creators and audiences to explore different facets of life. By dissecting the structural elements and thematic concerns specific to each genre, we gained valuable insights into the versatility of drama as a medium of expression.

A critical aspect of our journey has been the emphasis on performance as a dynamic drama component. The transition from page to stage brings dramatic works to life, transforming written words into powerful visual and auditory experiences. Through our discussions on acting techniques, stagecraft, and directorial vision, we recognised the collaborative nature of theatrical productions and the myriad ways in which performances can shape the audience's interpretation of the text. This understanding underscores the significance of viewing drama not solely as literary artefacts but as live, evolving art forms that engage all senses.

One of the most vital takeaways from this book is the value of critical analysis in enhancing our appreciation of dramatic texts. By applying analytical techniques such as close reading, thematic analysis, and contextual examination, we move beyond passive consumption to active engagement with the material. This process allows us to uncover deeper meanings, question assumptions, and draw connections between the text and the broader cultural and historical landscape. As we demonstrated through various examples, the ability to dissect the elements of a play transforms our interaction with it, turning a simple viewing experience into an insightful exploration of artistic intent and societal reflection.

Beyond the immediate context of the book, the skills and insights gained here pave the way for continued exploration of drama. The world of dramatic literature is vast and varied, encompassing works from different cultures and historical periods. With the foundational knowledge acquired, readers are encouraged to venture beyond familiar territories and discover lesser-known gems that offer new perspectives on universal themes. Exploring works from diverse cultural contexts, such as Indian Natya Shastra or African storytelling traditions, enriches our understanding of drama's global impact and capacity to bridge cultural divides.

Reflecting on the evolution of drama, we see a remarkable journey from ancient rituals to contemporary theatre. Despite the changes in form and presentation, the essence of drama—its ability to reflect society and probe the depths of the human condition—remains steadfast. This continuity amid innovation highlights the enduring power of drama to inspire, challenge, and connect people across time and space. Understanding this historical trajectory enriches our appreciation of modern theatrical experiences, reminding us that every performance we witness is part of a centuries-old storytelling tradition.

In conclusion, our exploration of drama has underscored its significance as a multifaceted art form that offers profound insights into the human experience. By revisiting the key themes and concepts discussed in each chapter, we reinforced the idea that drama's value lies not just in its entertainment potential but in its capacity to illuminate the complexities of life. Through critical analysis, we deepen our engagement with dramatic texts, transforming them into tools for reflection and understanding. The journey does not end here; with the skills and knowledge gained from this book, readers are well-equipped to continue exploring the boundless world of drama, discovering new works, and appreciating the rich legacy of this timeless art form.

To Readers

If you've found ***NEP Students Guide for Understanding Drama*** *helpful in your journey of exploring and appreciating dramatic works, I would be immensely grateful if you could take a moment to share your thoughts in a review of at least a couple of paragraphs on platforms like Amazon.in, Goodreads, or Instagram. Your feedback helps me improve and guides other readers in their own exploration of drama. Potential buyers of the book will appreciate your honest review. If you feel it's deserved, a positive review would be deeply appreciated as it encourages others to dive into this fascinating subject confidently. I appreciate your support!*

Thank you!

www.ingramcontent.com/pod-product-compliance
Ingram Content Group UK Ltd.
Pitfield, Milton Keynes, MK11 3LW, UK
UKHW062305290726
14090UKWH00018B/892